BUSINESS ISSUES, COMPETITION AND ENTREPRENEURSHIP

MULTINATIONAL'S CSR PRACTICES IN DEVELOPING COUNTRIES

AN INTERNATIONAL PERSPECTIVE

BUSINESS ISSUES, COMPETITION AND ENTREPRENEURSHIP

Additional books in this series can be found on Nova's website under the Series tab.

Additional e-books in this series can be found on Nova's website under the e-book tab.

BUSINESS ISSUES, COMPETITION AND ENTREPRENEURSHIP

MULTINATIONAL'S CSR PRACTICES IN DEVELOPING COUNTRIES

AN INTERNATIONAL PERSPECTIVE

ALIDOU OUEDRAOGO
EDITOR

nova publishers
New York

Library of Congress Cataloging-in-Publication Data

Multinational's CSR practices in developing countries : an international perspective / editor: Alidou Ouedraogo (University of Moncton, Canada).
       pages cm
  Includes index.
  ISBN 978-1-63463-479-3 (hardcover)
  1. Social responsibility of business. 2. International business enterprises--Moral and ethical aspects. 3. Corporations--Moral and ethical aspects. 4. Social responsibility of business--Case studies. 5. International business enterprises--Moral and ethical aspects--Case studies. 6. Corporations--Moral and ethical aspects--Case studies. I. Ouidraogo, Alidou.
  HD60.M854 2014
  658.4'08--dc23
  2014042355

Published by Nova Science Publishers, Inc. † New York

CONTENTS

Acknowledgments   vii

Introduction   1
       A. Ouedraogo

Chapter 1   A Plea for a Chinese Model of Ethical Leadership   **43**
       A. Barraquier

Chapter 2   Case Study: Renault Plant in Tangiers (Morocco)   **59**
       Alidou Ouedraogo

Chapter 3   MNCS and Anti-Corruption Practices: An Overview   **89**
       M. Shater Jannati

Chapter 4   The Business Case CSR for the World Market
       Leader in Brick Production
       (Wienerberger Tumkur Site – India)   **99**
       M. Neureiter

Chapter 5   The Need for a Finer Grained Analysis of the CSR
       of MNC Subsidiaries in Developing Countries   **105**
       D. Jamali

Chapter 6   Corporate Charity and Profitability   **117**
       D. Crowther and S. Seifi

Chapter 7   Labour Rights in Global Supply Chains:
       An Oxfam Case Study of Unilever in Vietnam   **137**
       R. Wilshaw and E. Sahan

Chapter 8   MNCS in Bangladesh: Adding Value through CSR   **159**
M. Babar

Editor's Contact Information   **167**

Index   **169**

ACKNOWLEDGMENTS

I have earned the gratitude of several institutions and individuals while pursuing this book. This work has gone through several stages of reviews, and it is a much better valuable product now. The enormous contribution by colleagues has to be appreciated at the outset. It is true that the goals of this book did get transformed during this period and that required some extra effort. However, the incorporation of many more issues and perspectives may have added to the relevance of this book. Readers will have to judge whether justice has been done to various viewpoints and perspectives adequately.

First, I would like to thank one special person: Patrick J. Gilabert, UNIDO representative in Vietnam. Patrick co-edited this book with me. He is a consummate professional and always committed to an inclusive and sustainable industrial development (ISID) of all developing countries. Comments and suggestions from Patrick were most valuable and in many cases have added enormous value to the quality of the book. There is no doubt that without his constant prodding and helpful chidings, this book would not have been completed. I should also thank Patrick's team which provided extensive coordination and assistance during the preparation of the book, Mrs. Maryam Shater Jannati, from Bocconi University Italy and Mr. Samuel Monteiro from CERDI Auvergne University France.

Second, I must thank large number of creative colleagues who were also very helpful: Anne Barraquier (SKEMA Business School, France), Maryam S. Jannati (Junior Officer, UNIDO-Vietnam), M. Neureiter (CEO, The CSR Company International, Vienna, Austria), Dima Jamali (Olayan School of Business, American University of Beirut, Lebanon), D. Crowther and S. Seifi (De Montfort University, United Kingdom and University Putra Malaysia, Malaysia), R. Wilshaw and E. Sahan (Ethical Trade Manager, Oxfam Great

Britain and Private Sector Policy Advisor, Oxfam Great Britain), M. Babar (CSR consultant and CEO, BizCare, Bangladesh).

I must also thank my colleagues from HEC Montréal, University of Moncton, University of Western Ontario, University of Quebec and University of Ottawa, and many others for helpful comments at various stage of the book and evolution of the ideas presented in this book.

I have earned the gratitude of many others while pursuing this book. Samuel Monteiro (junior officer at UNIDO-Vietnam) had to handle hundreds of mails on the subject, and organize every detail of papers and other aspects of the internal logistics, and do so many other things all, at once and that too without any mistake. I cannot imagine completing this book without his help. In addition my assistant and former graduate student Youssef Benghazouani and several others unnamed ones deserve thanks.

I am grateful to Professor Gaston Leblanc, dean and Professor Vivi Koffi, head of management department at the University of Moncton for excellent institutional support.

Finally, I must thank my family (my wife Maty and my son Kaysan) who kept patience with my long hours at work and never once complained in deference to the claims of those who have shared their knowledge with us and but are still to get their due.

Alidou Ouedraogo, Ph.D.
Professor of Management
University of Moncton (Canada)

INTRODUCTION

A. Ouedraogo[1]

[1]Professor, University of Moncton, Canada

On Monday October 31st 2011, the Secretary General of the United Nations, at a press conference in New York, offered a warm welcome to the seventh billionth inhabitant of our planet. Regardless of his nationality, he was born "in a world of terrible contradictions". "In what kind of world was this seventh billionth man born into?" What kind of planet will we bequeath to our children? [...] I am one of the seven billion. All of you are as well. Together we can ensure that these seven billion people are strong by working in unison for a better world for all.[1]" In his declaration, Ban Ki-moon renewed his wish to see a global endeavour by all participants working towards a better world. Governments, organizations, individuals, etc., are all invited to contribute to the effort.

Among the players called to action are corporate entities because of their role in the creation of wealth and the distribution of revenue, along with improving the wellbeing of individuals by offering them beneficial products that respond to their needs. Their footprint is quite palpable and consequential, whether it concerns the reduction of CO_2 emissions, biodiversity, access to potable water, waste management, or the taking into account of human rights and professional equality, establishing dialogue with other players, and

---

[1] Radio-Canada with Agence France-Presse and the Associated Press, Tuesday, November 1st, 2011.

addressing human suffering in the workplace. In addition, the many other subjects or themes that repeatedly appear are naturally undertaken by organizations (Dupuis et al., 2010). Henceforth, the responsibility of companies will be demonstrated by their actions in terms of reducing or suppressing negative external reviews (Tahari, 2008); we now count in the thousands companies who are signatories of the *Global Compact*.

The *Global Compact* is an initiative launched in 1999 on an impulse by M. Kofi Annan, Secretary-General of the United Nations at that moment. The pact creates a federation between corporate entities, the United Nations, and societal players that espouse fundamental values inspired by four important themes:

- The Universal Declaration of Human Rights (1948);
- Rio Declaration on Environment and Development (1992);
- (ILO) Declaration on Fundamental Principles and Rights at Work (1998);
- United Nations Convention against Corruption (2004);

These values are stated in ten universal principles that companies or organizations (UN, NGO, cities, institutions, etc.) have signed as part of the *Global Compact* and have promised to apply (Labaronne and Gana-Oueslati, 2011). By November 2010, more than 6,000 companies had signed as well as 1,955 other types of participants in more than 130 countries[2]. The ten principles of the Global Compact are grouped into four fields: human rights, rights of workers, environment, and fight against corruption (Table 1).

The basic foundation is the following: a company does not exist solely as a self-sufficient entity. It acts and interacts within an evolving environment susceptible of affecting it and, in return, affected by it (Reynaud and Papillon, 2003; Thompson, 2003; Astley and Fombrun, 1983; Aldrich, 1979; Hannan and Freeman, 1977). Faced with this axiom, we cannot deny that the company is a major player in society and that its management depends on values acceptable to its working environment as it is to the human and social axioms (Quairel and Capron, 2004). As well, the pressures exerted by stakeholder participants increasingly influence the decision makers and renders their work even more complex (Branco and Rodrigues, 2007; Quairel and Capron, 2004).

---

[2]Annual report (2010) of the Global Compact that we can find on the site: www.unglobalcompact.org.

Table 1. The Ten Principles of the Global Compact

Human rights	
Principle 1:	Businesses should support and respect the protection of internationally proclaimed human rights.
Principle 2:	Businesses should make sure they are not complicit in human rights abuses.
Labour	
Principle 3:	Businesses should uphold the freedom of association and the effective recognition of the right to collective bargaining.
Principle 4:	The elimination of all forms of forced and compulsory labor.
Principle 5:	The effective abolition of child labor.
Principle 6:	The elimination of discrimination in respect of employment and occupation.
Environment	
Principle 7:	Businesses should support a precautionary approach to environmental challenges.
Principle 8:	Businesses should undertake initiatives to promote greater environmental responsibility.
Principle 9:	Businesses should encourage the development and diffusion of environmentally friendly technologies.
Anti-corruption	
Principle 10:	Businesses should work against corruption in all its forms, including extortion and bribery.

It is in this light that the notion of Corporate Social Responsibility[3] (CSR) was developed (Bowen, 1953; Carroll, 1979). This concept stipulates that the aim of any organization is not solely to satisfy a single category of the interested stakeholders[4] (Freeman, 1984) as an automatic default (deference) to shareholders, but to have a larger vision that incorporates other parties concerned by its actions and resistance to corruption during the process for choosing future orientations. Between the reality proposed, with a sign of voluntary compliance, and the strategies of superficial conformity that are apparent and opportunistic, higher stakes develop in terms of transparency,

---

[3]In 1953, Bowen, an economist and protestant pastor, published "Responsibility of the business man". He was the first to use the term "Corporate Social Responsibility", later called "Social Responsibility of Companies"

[4]During the 1960s, the term "stakeholder" emerged. Popularized by Freeman (1984), the term is often referred to as "stakeholder party", but also as "interested party" or "having a right".

risk, and reputation (Cardebat and Cassagnard, 2009; Capron and Quairel, 2004).

As newer methods for piloting and evaluating appear, thereby combining different elements of responsibility along with the association of stakeholders, we find a whole new range of management tools (*i.e.* code of conduct, social, and environmental norms and certifications, societal reports, notes, etc.). These must be stripped down to basics and analysed in order to obtain a better understanding of this concept and its associated practices, in a new context where CSR now appears to be an open, multiform idea under construction (Acquier and Gond, 2007, Acquier and Aggeri, 2006; Aggeri et al., 2005; Gond, 2006).

This approach will be very useful in our attempt to understand the methodology of corruption in such a concept in order to answer our issues. At this point, we are interested in knowing at which level CSR will be acknowledged and accepted in a context other than its origins and place of predilection; specifically, North America and Europe (Acquier and Gond, 2007; Pasquero, 2005).

In other words, is the concept of transferability towards developing countries conceivable? Are local companies prepared and equipped to integrate it in their approach? In case of offshore relocation, will multinational companies apply the principles of this concept in the host countries? If so, what particularities or nuances must we take into account?

AIM OF THIS BOOK

Organizations today must evolve in a world of perpetual change. Convictions once held in the past are no longer necessarily those that are held today; as well, over the past twenty years companies have been immersed in a crisis environment (Martinet and Payaud, 2011; Dupuis et al., 2010). Thus, the recurring crises that we are accustomed to, due to upheavals in the financial, economical, social, and ecological fields, highlight the CSR in our society, and is therefore usurping one of the neoliberal dogmas that stipulates "*the responsibility of companies is to make a profit to enrich shareholders*[5]".

Besides, the crisis signals a rupture with former commonly accepted values, upheavals in known production processes, and confrontation with competitors (Martinet and Payaud, 2011; Dupuis et al., 2010). Hence, the

---

[5] A summary of the famous formula by Milton Friedman presented in 1970.

emergence of the notion of CSR modifies considerably the range of indicators to take into account to measure the value created or destroyed by organizations. Consequently, there is a growing need for reliable information on the extra-financial performance of these organizations (Dupuis et al., 2010, Dohou-Renaud and Berland, 2007).

Furthermore, the relationship between organizations and markets has undergone a profound transformation and once forceful relationships are no longer the same (Cochoy, 2002). Throughout these years, consumers, in particular, had seen their negotiating power and their influence increase considerably by profiting from a shortage based economy to a society of abundance (Bertin and Clement, 2007; Kornai, 1980, 1984; Galbraith, 1958; Beck, 1986; Schulze, 1993).

Progressively, the consumer himself became the center of preoccupation by companies and subsequently by CSR departments as such (Duong and Robert-Demontrond, 2004). He seeks to obtain a personal advantage for himself and his immediate surroundings; however, few consumers relate spontaneously CSR to companies or even entire certain sectors. Education and healthcare nevertheless are identified as being the most responsible sectors from a societal point of view; nonetheless, CSR does not produce a value-added number for the consumer unless it is pertinent and is seen as a recovery in the policies of the product and the brand name of the company. In these recessionary times, it is remarkable to see the extent at which consumers appreciate profitable companies... These are a few of the interesting conclusions in the study "Corporate Social Responsibility" realized by InSites Consulting via discussion groups that were created across the world (Geers, 2009).

Paradoxically, other researchers observed a "resistance by consumers to social labelling". From criticism of the methods to criticism of the "underlying economic logic", the objective of this study has been the emergence of CSR resistance movements (Demontrond and Joyeau, 2010). By relying on two qualitative empirical studies conducted between 2006 and 2008, they analysed the phenomenon that emerged as a reaction to the policies of the CSR implemented by companies for a number of years.

The study conducted reveals two crises of legitimacy for CSR. The first, which stems from the example of initiating label diversity, is listed in a register for denouncing the sincerity of voluntary company initiatives. The second type of criticism, based on an analysis of fair trade, stems from the refusal of players to admit that the defense and promotion of ethical values can have a place in the organization of traditional companies (Demontrond and Joyeau, 2010).

We view these dealings or negotiations as being very interesting. Between those who believe it and those who doubt it (Friedman, 1970; Levitte, 1958), the arguments are equally solid on both sides of this divide. Numerous studies were undertaken to judge and gage the impact of CSR, its degree of integration at organizational levels, the results, and on their competitive advantage (Porter and Kramer, 2006, McWilliams, Siegel and Wright, 2005).

In this way, the authors presented models of contingency factors susceptible of explaining the links between CSR and economic performance (Rowley and Berman, 2000). For example, in its report published in 2002, the European Commission, after receiving replies from companies on its Green Book[6] presented in 2001, recognized that said replies reflected a larger consensus on the strategic importance that will provide the means for CSR to establish commercial success, especially in the long term.

It is also interesting to note that multinational companies (MNC) are the first to be doubted as to their real intentions. In fact, the negative opinion of the authenticity of CSR strategies, which have always been suspected of favoring, first and foremost, the image of innovative companies or to view growth only in terms of the number of consumers in the host region or country, represents a genuine challenge (Martinet and Payaud, 2011). Having first appeared in northern countries, the very notion of CSR still remains vague in developing countries. Nevertheless, studies exist on the CSR of multinationals in third world countries, such as the report by the OECD in 2008 that examined the social impact of direct outside investment in the host countries.

These studies came to light after controversies, fueled by the schemes or machinations by MNC, generated uneasiness with public opinion. They are accused of unfair competition, for example, because they profit from low salaries and difficult working conditions as observed in certain foreign countries. They are also accused of violating human rights and the rights of workers in developing countries where governments do not consistently respect these rights (Report OECD, 2008).

---

[6]In July 2001, the European Commission edited its Green Book regarding CSR entitled "Promoting a European framework for "Corporate Social Responsibilities." By publishing this green book, the European Commission brought the discussion of CSR to an international level. It was a first step towards a larger dialogue between the institutions of different countries. This Green Book was followed by two other updated communications in 2002 and 2006.
A résumé is available at the following address: http://rse-pro.com/rse-livre-vert-183

In numerous OECD countries, the public sector and others have consistently called upon MNC to apply the same standards enforced in their country of origin to all their foreign divisions and subsidiaries. Hence, the *head office – subsidiary relationship* is of utmost importance when it comes to social responsibility (Pestre, 2007). Despite the fact that such CSR behaviour has improved among companies; unfortunately, it is insufficient, and therefore must be included in any regulatory framework (Stiglitz, 2006).

That being said, we must remember that multinational companies are not the only ones affected. Depending on the country, there exists an economic social fabric comprised of local companies, both public and private, that must in turn take over from CSR and act in a socially responsible way. During the last decade, researchers have looked at this question and have attempted to better understand such a phenomenon. At first, some examined this question in the context of developing countries (Jamali and Mirshak, 2007), while others questioned the role of local companies (Boutti, 2009; Gherib et al., 2009; M'hamdi and Trid, 2009; Tahari, 2008) as well as the institutional framework that either favors or not the advent of socially responsible companies (Labaronne and Gana-Oueslati, 2011).

In spite of divergent opinions between those who view CSR as a vehicle for both human and economic development, and those who view it with a cynical eye filled with doubt, and believing that it is a vile tool for exploitation, restraining growth, and a sort of protectionism in disguise; it goes without saying that regardless of viewpoints, local companies must fully embrace the concept, adapt it, and consequently contribute to the economic development and growth of their country.

PART 1: THEORETICAL FOUNDATIONS OF CSR

1.1. CSR: Early Evolution and Economic Expansion

1.1.1. Evolution of CSR

The term responsibility comes from the Latin "respondere" which means "to be guarantor of". The vocal word "responsabilité" is also defined in the Le Petit Robert dictionary as the "obligation to repair the damage that one has created by his own fault in certain cases as determined by law". If one relies on the sense conferred by the term responsibility, then CSR should, therefore, bind a company and its obligation towards its entourage.

Though presented, at times, as a novel idea of the last decade, the concept of CSR is, in actual fact, an integral part of a long tradition of discussion, based on practical knowledge, on the relationships between the private sector and Society, which dates back to at least the beginning of the 20th century in North America (Acquier and Gond, 2007; D'Humière and Chauveau, 2001). We have said "at least" because there are researchers that claim that, despite the fact that the terms that we have used in the past to designate social responsibility were different than the terms used today, it is possible to follow the different types and examples of social responsibility throughout the centuries back to the period of classical Athens (500 BC) under the guise of heroic events (Rodić, 2007; Nikos, 2004). As for Pasquero (2005), he goes back even further in antiquity and refers to the Code of Hammurabi[7] XVIII centuries BC.

It would also be misleading to believe that CSR is purely "American". The concern for social issues is not a contemporary capitalistic prerogative. Already in nineteenth century England, Germany, and France, certain industrialists had distinguished themselves by their social preoccupations: lodging, social insurance, charitable donations towards workers and their families, etc. Likewise, certain religious congregations or socialist thinkers had imagined alternative manufacturing facilities where community spirit and the territorial attachment already had their place (Acquier and Gond, 2007; Segal, 2003; Epstein, 2002).

As such, with the dawn of the 20th century and the widespread enactment of laws and social protection programs, this charitable spirit receded to make room for very large legislative projects, both conventional and institutional. After the Second World War, with the advent of a new "era of organizers" (Burnham, 1947), the incredible growth in the size of American industrial

---

[7]Hammurabi reigned over Babylon from 1795 to 1750 BC. It was he himself who built the grandeur of a cosmopolitan city today recognized as the first metropolis in human history. He decreed a set of laws, and had them engraved on a stone that he exposed in the heart of the city. This stone was discovered in 1901. It is the most ancient complete code known, although we know that he was inspired by more ancient texts. Among the 282 articles, a large number concern what we would call today commercial law, that is, the rights and (especially) the duties of different "wealthy" economic parties of the time.

Besides its anecdotal aspect, the reference to the Hammurabi Code invites reflections concerning the necessity for a complex society to give itself common rules for sound economic behaviour. For defenders of CSR, it represents an unavoidable argument to establish the legitimacy of the concept based on an historical permanent record from any concern to define the role and responsibilities of the economic players since antiquity. The CSR is therefore nothing more than transposing to the liberal capitalistic world what the Hammurabi Code was for a despotic world in ancient times (Pasquero, 2005).

companies (Chandler, 1988), the arrival of multinational firms and their growing role in the world economy will, taken together, once again force us to ask about the nature of the relationship between companies and society, and the responsibilities of its directors regarding the latter (Acquier and Gond, 2007).

In this way, therefore, we found ourselves to be in a favourable context regarding the emergence of the notion of CSR supported by philosophical, ethical, and pragmatic reasons, in addition to profiting from established ground towards a new era (Pasquero, 2005). For, even if other countries could realize similar historical conditions for economic development, it was not by chance that the actual conceptual form of CSR was developed in the United-States. American society was, in effect, a particularly opportune testing ground for this type of experiment. Once begun, four socio-cultural factors contributed to maintaining it steadfast and viable: individualism, democratic pluralism, morals, and utilitarianism (Pasquero, 2005, 2004, 1997).

All of these factors will have their own highlights and will be translated through the work of an economist and pastor, Howard R. Bowen, who is often identified as the founder of this discipline (Pasquero, 2005; Carroll, 1999, 1979; Wood, 1991). In fact, his book published in 1953, Social Responsibilities of the Businessman is considered a fundamental work, anticipating and structuring the theoretical approaches to matters of CSR (Acquier and Gond, 2007).

1.1.2. The Conceptual Evolution of CSR

1.1.2.1. Years 1950/1960: Beginning of a New Era in Social Responsibility

The first studies on CSR were focused on the evaluation of the outline of this phenomenon. It is at this time that the expression for CSR appears for the first time, defined as being compliant to "*pursue the policies, make the decisions, or follow the desired path in terms of the objectives and the values of our Society*[8]". Consequently, those studies were seeking to determine the responsibilities of capitalistic companies regarding their effects on society (Rodić, 2007; Pasquero, 2005, Caroll, 1999).

In his works, Bowen insisted that the contribution by industry was essential in order to strengthen the American dream's values that were within reach. As such, he joins the protestant work ethic that stipulates that a good

---

[8]Translation proposed by Acquier and Gond (2007) and Bowen, 1953, p. 6.

entrepreneur shall behave as the head of a family, managing profits in a responsible manner, thrifty, and without ostentation. Industry is thus seen as an equal social participant, thereby entrusted with the same goals towards society at large (Dupuis et al., 2010; Delbard, 2009).

Since then, the definition of societal responsibility has noticeably evolved over time. In 1960, Keith Davis attempted to formalize, or at least define in a concrete manner, the concept of CSR (Carroll, 1991). He suggests that social responsibility is the result of the decisions and actions taken by company directors for reasons that go beyond purely economic or technical decisions[9] (Dohou-Renaud and Berland, 2007).

During this stage, in the 50s and 60s, the objectives were becoming more of a philanthropic effort whose primary motivation was moral respect. There was no clear strategy; rather it was an *ad hoc* approach. The initiator was principally the administrator and the concept functioned according to a principle of passiveness. In addition, there was no follow-up or any control conducted by a third party (Rodić, 2007; Pasquero, 2005; Caroll, 1999).

1.1.2.2. The 1970s: Proliferation of Definitions for Corporate Social Responsibility

A particular line of thinking concentrated on the way industry could concretely detect and manage the problems of CSR pertinent to them. This approach leads to favoring a more procedural vision and to working on the concept of social sensitization by industry (Rodić, 2007, Caroll, 1999).

In his article *"Corporate Social Responsibility: Evolution of a Definitional Construct"*, Caroll (1999) prepares a list that one could qualify as exhaustive of the authors who contributed to the evolution of the CSR concept. He himself will attempt to provide a definition. In 1979, Carroll thus defines the notion of societal responsibility as *"what society expects from organizations in economic, legal, ethical, and discretionary matters"*. His works have merit by combining the different aspects of responsibility, clarifying this notion, and highlighting the expectations expressed vis-à-vis organizations (Dohou-Renaud and Berland, 2007).

Again from Caroll (1999), the major work of this period stems from the *"Committee for Economic Development"* (CED). In 1971, the CED enlarged the concept of CSR by referring to three concentric circles as follows: *"the first includes the basic responsibilities in order to accomplish the essential*

---

[9]Davis will become better known during the 70s and 80s for his vision of the relationship between social responsibility and business leaders (Carroll, 1991).

functions of the company relative to production, employment, and economic growth; the second encompasses the first but includes a broader notion of responsibility with greater sensitivity towards an evolving society and its requirements by taking into consideration concerns regarding environmental protection, social relationships, or even providing consumer information; and, finally, the third takes into consideration the management of emerging responsibilities that serve to improve the environment by creating employment opportunity to profit particularly underprivileged populations" (Germain and Trébucq, 2004, p. 36, citations by Dohou-Renaud and Berland, 2007).

1.1.2.3. The 1980s/1990s: Fewer Definitions, More Research and Alternative Themes

In the 1980s, another vision of corporations emerged; one that considered that industry is not only responsible to the owner shareholders, but also to all the stakeholder participants involved: employees, suppliers, clients, and territories (Freeman, 1984). This new vision marked a turning point in the sense of a more open, approachable and discerning industry (Dupuis et al., 2010; Rodić, 2007; Caroll, 1999).

Moreover, other concepts or themes that appeared, largely generated by the debate on CSR, are mentioned as well. At that moment in time, ideas discussed were: Sensitivity or the Social Receptiveness of Companies[10], Public Policy of Companies, Ethical Affairs, stakeholder participants … (Caroll, 1999).

Furthermore, the 1990s were marked by a weakening of the United Nations, a growing globalization, dissolution of the compromise with Fordism, and a declining image of large companies (environmental catastrophes, work-related accidents, layoff of workers etc.) This set of factors contributed in turn to the development of the concept of CSR (Dupuis et al., 2010; Rodić, 2007; Caroll, 1999).

In itself, the need existed to arrive at a definition for societal performance by industry. In addition, there was a need to provide answers repeatedly to a pressing issue: What are the "ethical" principles of corporate entities and how do corporations concretely implement its principles? It follows that a more vigorous and thought-out approach should be considered (Rodić, 2007).

---

[10]Our translation of: Corporate Social Responsiveness

1.1.2.4. The 2000s: Geographical Dispersal

At the turn of the century, the CSR concept makes a remarkable entrance on the European scene, in part because of a series of initiatives by the European Commission (European Commission, 2001). White papers are published, forums are organized, and inter-university research networks are created.

Thirty years after America, Europe finally takes *seriously* the concept of CSR (Pasquero, 2005). The CSR concept seems therefore appropriate considering the logical relationship between the grand humanistic principles and the daily practices of companies, and in so doing evolves from the philosophy of utopian effectiveness to one of strategic actions (Pasquero, 2005).

This period is characterized by companies identifying the extraneous financial factors that will allow them to contribute to sustainable development without sacrificing their economic performance (Rodić, 2007; Pasquero, 2005). Moreover, throughout the world, even in the least developed countries, the concept of CSR takes root, even if "... *it is usually at the discussion level. However, more and more entrepreneurs are realizing that social irresponsibility has a limited time span in business, for eventually the day will come where past negligent behaviour will ultimately cost them considerably more in capital expenses and social intangibles*" (Pasquero, 2005).

Having presented the conceptual evolution of CSR, it should be noted that there is still no consensus on the definition for CSR (M'hamdi and Trid, 2009). Even in 2008, more than 50 years after the initial concept, Dahlsrud proposes a very interesting analysis of at least 37 definitions currently in use to describe the term[11]. In fact, "the term CSR has been used as a synonym for business ethics defined as the equivalent of a philanthropic corporation and is considered strictly tied to environmental policies. The lack of consistency in the use of the term CSR makes it difficult to compare the results of research papers that are published, thus hindering our capacity to understand the implications of CSR activities. We are hoping for the emergence of a common definition acceptable for the CSR[12]" (Mc Williams et al., 2005).

---

[11]To consult all of the definitions, we suggest that you look at the table in the appendix of the article published by Dahlsrud (2008), *How Corporate Social Responsibility Is Defined: An Analysis of 37 Definitions. Corporate Social Responsibility and Environmental Management* 15 (1)

[12]Our translation of *McWilliams, Siegel and Wright, 2005, Corporate Social Responsibility: Strategic Implications, paragraph on Theoretical issues to be resolved.*

We believe that there is confusion, notably on three points: confusion in the conceptualization (definitions of CSR by different players involved – industry, rating agencies, and researchers); confusion in the specific operational needs of CSR variables and other variables used to measure the effects of CSR (social performance and financial performance); and finally confusion in the exploitation and the implementation of social reporting by industry (different facets of expression and analysis of CSR in reports) (Allouche et al., 2004).

For the sake of clarity, we will nonetheless provide the two most widely used definitions in the world according to Dahlsrud (2008). The first is the way by which the European Commission in its Green Book defines CSR, specifically as "the voluntary integration by industry of the social and environmental preoccupations related to their commercial activities and their relationship with their stakeholder partners[13]".

The second definition is proposed by the "The World Business Council for Sustainable Development" (WBCSD) that presents the CSR as "a continuous commitment by industry to act correctly on ethical matters and to contribute to economic development, while improving the quality of life for its employees and their families, the local community, and society[14] as a whole."

1.1.3. The CSR: Existence of a Counter-Current

Our review of literature would be considered incomplete if we did not discuss the counter current. In fact, the concept of CSR is far from being unanimous. Moreover, it would be particularly interesting to mention that Bowen, during his time as director of the economics department at the University of Illinois, had to face a conservative counter-current when he decided to integrate the teaching of CSR in the degree course at the same university. His decisions in terms of teaching and the evaluation of researchers, judged too antinomic with neo-classical approaches, guaranteed him the wrath and fury of many to the point where he had to resign[15] (Acquier and Gond, 2007).

Theodore Levitt is considered as the first to have initiated a debate on the question in his article "*The Dangers of Social Responsibility*" published in

---

[13]Green Book, Promote a European framework for the social responsibility of companies COM (2001) 366 final, 18 July 2001

[14]See: www.wbcsd.org

[15]Acquier and Gond (2007) remind us that this episode is known under the name "Bowen controversy" that leads to the resignation of the latter in 1950, just before the publication of his major work "Social Responsibilities of the Businessman".

1958 (McWilliams et al., 2005). With such a provocative title, he states that the work of government and that of industry managers are totally different[16]. Milton Friedman (1970) expressed the same aversion and added that the existence of CSR is the sign of an agency problem within the organization (McWilliams et al., 2005).

According to Friedman, the agency theory implies that CSR is synonymous with using inefficient resources from the organization, and that we benefit more by investing them in projects having an intrinsic value-added element or by simply returning the profits to shareholders. He also argues that the CSR is a springboard used by management staff for advancing their career or suiting their personal agenda.

More recently, other authors have criticized the concept of CRS with the same cynicism. Banerjee[17] (2008) argued that despite the rhetoric on CRS and the citizen society, these concepts exist only to serve the interests of shareholders while hindering the stakeholder parties. He proposes an alternative perspective to the concept by considering it as an ideological movement aimed at legitimizing and consolidating the power of large firms. Devinney[18] (2009) continues on the same path and does not hesitate to qualify the notion of CRS as an *oxymoron*[19] because of the conflicting nature of industry itself. The two authors agree on the naivety of those who believe that companies are guided by society and not by their own profits.

For Devinney, the socially responsible enterprise is simply impossible (Devinney, 2009). He argues that we must accept that, as a social organism, industry is a complex hybrid of virtue and vices that cannot be separated. In other words, companies are like individuals, who are constantly in conflict. Consequently, if we grant private sector companies the power to make social decisions, we must accept the fact that they will use this power in a manner that they deem appropriate and we will have to accept it regardless if we disagree (Devinney, 2009).

In summary, this section allowed us to examine the outline of the notions regarding CSR by citing the principal evolutionary stages that the concept has

---

[16]"Government's job is not business, and business's job is not government". *The Dangers of Social Responsibility*, 1958, p. 47. Citation by Mc Williams, Siegel and Wright, 2005

[17]Banerjee (2007) "*Corporate Social Responsibility: The Good, the Bad and the Ugly.*"

[18]Devinney (2009) "*Is the Socially Responsible Corporation a Myth? The Good, the Bad, and the Ugly of Corporate Social Responsibility?*"

[19]In rhetoric, an oxymora or oxymoron, from the Greek ὀξύμωρος (oxúmōros - de ὀξύς, "sharp, spiritual, end", and from μωρός, "naive, stupid", which means "clever, stupid, spiritual as per an apparent stupidity") is a figure of speech that aims to coalesce two terms (noun and adjective) whose sense should be opposite, in a form that appears contradictory.

seen from its origins to this date. As such, we have a concept of strong altruistic connotations, but also one that incurs mistrust due to the underlying financial logic and the propaganda that it suggests.

Numerous studies and research have been conducted to evaluate the impact of CSR on the global performance of organizations. As a result, the data obtained varies considerably between the existence of a positive, neutral, and even negative correlation between the two variables. The major reason for these disparities was explained above: the absence of a unanimous definition of the concept. Consequently, we have differences in the choice of models for analysis of corporate performance, the choice of samples etc.

It is true that CSR, in the beginning, evolved from an imprecise conceptual stage to a theoretical adequacy test stage with a more progressive vision; secondly, in qualitative terms, there was a significant growth in the total number of studies dedicated to this subject matter; and finally the CSR and the social performance (SP), epistemological speaking, tend to converge as concepts treating the same problem (Herrera et al., 2011)[20].

However, we deplore the lack of knowledge concerning other aspects such as the appropriation of CSR concepts by SMBs (Lindgreen and Swaen, 2010). Until now, SMBs were more or less encouraged to be spectators of social activism and to concentrate on avoiding a *socially irresponsible* behaviour (M'hamdi and Trid, 2009).

One of the principal reasons put forth was the insignificant social impact that individual small businesses would have. In fact, when they are considered individually, SMBs have a significantly lower impact than that of large businesses where the consequences of a single decision may be devastating (M'hamdi and Trid, 2009).

Finally, although the CSR concept is part of the globalization of the world economy, research in this field remains largely localized. Hence, there is a necessity to undertake investigations regarding the perception and the practice of CSR in different contexts (Lee, 2008). Table 2 summarizes most of the CSR theoretical studies.

---

[20]Herrera, Alcañiz, Pérez and García (2011) conducted an analysis of the contents of 1082 articles published in the most widely regarded research publications between the periods 1972 to 2006 to arrive at these three conclusions.

Table 2. Selection of Theoretical Studies on CSR between 2006 and 2011

Author	Theoretical Perspective	Argument/Major Result
Porter and Kramer (2006)	Theory of the company	The CSR has become an inevitable priority for management because of pressure exerted by governments, activists, and the media. However, the efforts applied to the task are not as productive as they should be for two reasons: First, they present a business as an enemy of society when both are interdependent. Secondly, they force companies to examine the subject of CSR in a generic manner while they should be adapted to their own proper strategies.
Lee (2008)	Theory of the company	In terms of the level of analysis, researchers have moved on from a discussion of the macro-social effects to an analysis of the organizational level of CSR and its impact on the organizational and performance aspects. In theoretical terms, researchers changed their explicitly and normative arguments geared towards ethics, to implicitly normative managerial studies geared towards performance.
Sweeney and Coughlan (2008)	Theory of stakeholder parties	Organizations have increasingly had access to CSR activities (such as annual reports) to position their brands in the eyes of consumers and other stakeholder parties
Devinney (2009)	Institutionalize Theory	A socially responsible company is fundamentally impossible. We must accept that, as a social organism, the company must be a complex mix of virtues and vices that cannot be separated. Companies, like individuals, are naturally in conflict. If we grant companies the power to make social decisions, we must also accept the fact that they will use such power as they judge appropriate, and we could not reproach them if we were in disagreement.

Author	Theoretical Perspective	Argument/Major Result
Vlachos and Tsamakos (2011)	Theory of stakeholder parties	The study reveals a mediator role for consumer confidence in the evaluations framework on subjects related to CSR. To gain customer loyalty, management should attempt to lower the perception of grants motivated by profit, while in the attempt to recruit them, management should focus on building a perception of grants based on kindness and voluntarism.

Source: Adapted from McWilliams, Siegel and Wright (2005), Corporate Social Responsibility: Strategic Implications, Working Papers in Economics

1.2. The Corporate Social Responsibility: Theoretical Framework

Depending on the authors and their convictions, the theoretical framework of CSR will change accordingly. We consider useful to examine each one of these theories that represent the fundamental concepts of CSR. The intent of this section is to complete our review of the literature in order to gain insight on these hypotheses and to assist us in answering our problematic.

1.2.1. The Agency Theory

The separation between management control and the control of the capital of a company introduces a source of uncertainty that can take many forms. In effect, the directors of a company can decide to not maximize profit, and pursue other objectives. This phenomenon is possible in companies where the capital is widely held; consequently, a managerial power can emerge that can, in fact, impose its decisions on the shareholders. This type of control was brought to light for the first time by Berle and Means in 1932. Other studies will follow and show that directors cannot be simply summarized as managers seeking to maximize profit (Charreaux and Pitol-Belin, 1987; Demsetz, 1967).

The agency theory is so named from the agency relationship that creates a lien with the "principal" (he who delegates the decision-making) and the "agent". Because of divergent interests between the principals and the agents, asymmetrical information, and the incomplete nature of contracts, they incur agency costs and therefore a loss of value (Jensen and Meckling, 1976; Ross,

1973). The function of organizations and organizational mechanisms is to reduce this cost. In the agency theory, the company itself is a body of proof of agency relations (Charreaux and Pitol-Belin, 1987).

In general, this theory applies simultaneously to the architecture of the company and to the distribution of organizational forms. The results provided shed light on questions of centralization/decentralization, regulating the company, remuneration methods and performance measures as well as the governance of the companies.

1.2.2. The Stakeholder Theory

The role of a company, of its directors, and the nature of their obligations toward the rest of society is the subject of a long-standing debate. It is interesting to note that the approach of the *Stakeholder* is now seriously taking root, as was the case notably in the Agency Theory according to Berle and Means (1932). The latter observed the development of social pressure that is exerted on company directors so that they may recognize their responsibility towards all those whose well-being may be affected by decisions made by the company (Gond and Mercier, 2004).

It was during the 1960s that the term *Stockholder* took hold. According to Freeman (1984, 2010), it appeared for the first time in 1963 during a strategy review at the *Stanford Research Institute* (SRI) by Ansoff and Stewart. This neologism stems at the time from a deliberate desire to play with the term *Stockholder* (designating a shareholder) in order to indicate that other parties have an interest or stake in the company.

The *Stakeholder Theory* proposes an analysis of interactions that exist between the company and its extended environment at large. The Stakeholder Theory became one of the dominant theoretical references among the abundant literature concerning organizational ethics and the social responsibility of the company. It is also used increasingly in human resource management, notably, to grasp its contribution in organizational performance[21]. The evaluation of social performance of a company is based, increasingly, on the *Stakeholder* approach (Gond and Mercier, 2004).

However, as many authors have remarked, (Gond and Mercier, 2004; Phillips et al. 2003), the notion of *Stakeholder* does not have the same meaning for everyone. The different interpretations reflect the controversies concerning the rights attributed to *Stakeholders*. Thus, a larger vision of the notion of *Stakeholder* seems to present problems according to many authors,

---

[21]See Winstanley and Woodall, 2000; Greenwood, 2002 citation by Gond and Mercier, 2004.

since anyone could claim an interest in an organization, hence the necessity to accept a more limited definition of the concept (Gond and Mercier, 2004).

1.2.3. Resource-Based View of the Firm

The *Resource-Based View of the Firm (RBV)* states that companies possess resources, a sub-group that allows them to gain a competitive advantage, and another sub-group that leads to a better performance in the long-term. Thus, resources that are precious and rare may lead to the creation of a competitive advantage. This advantage can be maintained over long periods to the extent that the company is capable of protecting itself against the transfer, substitution, or imitation of the resources.

The RBV is the result of work done by Birger Wernerfelt. Although this approach was proposed for the first time in 1984, Wernerfelt realized that we did not begin to understand the full scope of his theory until 1990[22] (Wernerfelt, 1995). He himself summarized, in a synthetic way, his theory as follows: "a truism that organizations have a certain resource structure that governs its strategies and that it takes time and money to change the said structure." (Wernerfelt, 1995)

In his work, he attempted to observe companies as a function of their resources rather than their products. This perspective enlightens in a different way the strategic options that are available, particularly for companies having diverse activities. It is also interesting to see the analogy established between the principal of barriers to entry and the possession of resources on one hand; and between the resource/product matrices and the growth/market shares on the other hand.

1.2.4. The Institutional Theory

The institutional theory is very focused on the most profound aspects of the social structure. It considers that the processes by which the structures, including flow sheets, regulations, norms and routines are established as the main lines having authority over matters of social behaviour. It questions the way these elements are created, distributed, adopted and adapted over a period of time, and how they begin their decline and become obsolete (Scott and Richard, 2004).

---

[22]His article "A Resource based View of the Firm", published in 1984, received the award for *best paper published in the Strategic Management Journal* in 1994, a full 10 years later, as recognition for his work.

There is no unique or universal definition from official institutions as such. However, we can say that the institutions are social structures that have reached a high level of resistance. They are composed of cultural, cognitive, norms, and controls that together with activities and resources ensure stability and a purpose to the social dimensions (Scott, 1995, 2001).

These social structures are both imposed and later confirmed by means of the players' behaviour (individuals, organizations, etc.). It is cognitive, from one viewpoint, because a given institution is encoded by a player via a process of socialization. When it is interiorized, it transforms itself into a script (behaviour). When, or if, a player behaves himself according to the script, the institution is adopted. In this way, institutions are permanently produced. After a certain timeframe, the institution (and resulting behaviour) becomes sedimentary and taken for granted. Afterwards, it could be difficult for the players themselves to realize that their behaviour is, in fact, partly controlled by an institution. Acting in accordance with the institution is considered rationale (evidenced in itself) by those who share the institution (Bjorck, 2004).

1.2.5. The Theory of the Firm

A "Theory of the Firm" is a conceptual tool for explaining the firm as an object of analysis. Traditionally, this covers three aspects: the nature of the firm (What is a firm? What does the firm do? How is the firm created?), the boundaries of the firm (Where does it begin? Where does it end? Where does the market begin? Where do other firms begin?), and the internal organization of the firm (How is the firm organized? What are its structures? What are the organizational processes?) (Gindis, 2008).

For Ronald Coase (1937), the definition of the firm is that it is a "system of relationships controlled by the entrepreneur". Coase then attempts to show why the firm emerges as a market economy, in other words, why in an "ocean of unconscious coordination" (the market) there exists these "Islands of consciousness" (the firms) (Gindis, 2008).

Besides, the boundaries of the firm correspond to the perimeter of activities by the firm. Hence, the vertical integration identifies the passage of one group of inter-firm values to a group of intra-firm values. In other words, it is the passage of a market relationship (between supplier and clients) to a relationship of utilization. For Coase, in his perspective, the size of the firm will grow until the cost of supplementary integration equals the cost of the same transaction on the market (Gindis, 2008).

PART 2: CORPORATE SOCIAL RESPONSIBILITY IN DEVELOPING COUNTRIES

2.1. CSR: A Nomadic and Malleable Concept

Among the known important characteristics of the concept of CSR and associated concepts, we find their *nomadism* and their *malleability* (Acquier and Gond, 2007). The "nomadism" expresses the ease at which the players have at importing them in the context of very different interpretations. Regarding "malleability", it now allows us the possibility of reworking these notions to translate them as a function of the context thereby giving them a new meaning (Acquier and Gond, 2007). In short, these notions are considered as being "*elastic concepts*" (Aggeri et al., 2005), having a sufficient symbolic power to be largely dispersed throughout a given field, and based on general principles thus leaving room for local *re-appropriation* and *re-interpretation* (Acquier and Gond, 2007; Gond, 2006; Gond and Boxenbaum, 2004).

Already, Pasquero in 1997 had made the same observation by noting that the internationalization of the CSR concept followed two paradoxical tendencies. On one hand, he grants *universality* under the aegis of the multiplication of international norms. On the other hand, he grants *autonomy*, by allowing each country to acclimatize it to the local cultural and institutional conditions (Pasquero, 1997). Besides, Pasquero explains that if CSR is globalized, it is because it is supported by three amplifying factors whose action is also durable and universal (Pasquero, 2002):

- *A **libertarian thrust***, that manifests itself by a certain withdrawal of the State and an accent on the values of individual initiatives, but cannot be justified unless it is accompanied by an increase sense of responsibility.
- *A **technological thrust**,* whose rhythm is accelerating, but where the obvious profits are accompanied as well by increasingly new societal challenges, whether in the field of ethics (biogenetics), environmental issues (gashouse emissions), social (access to the Web), or policies (ownership conflicts).
- *A **Global thrust*** that generates problems that transcend political boundaries and cannot in the absence of global regulations that are still illusory, find solutions unless all the major players, including industry, accept the responsibilities and the consequences of their actions.

Nomad and malleable as it is, the concept of CSR is close to becoming universal without neglecting the local realities considering that it is subject to being adapted, thus inserting questions as to its applicability and consequently the ensuing results. The amplification factors discussed by Pasquero only confirm this tendency.

2.2. Developing Countries and CSR: Between Economic Development and Sustainable Development

2.2.1. The Measure of Economic Development

The word "development" is a very important concept when we discuss "countries undergoing development". A good indicator as to the degree of development, though still inadequate (Dobers and Halme, 2009), is provided by the "Human Development Index" (HDI) that combines monetary and non-monetary indicators of human development. It contains three elements: birthrate life expectancy, level of education and the alphabetization of adults, and the GDP per capita of the country. Thus, instead of looking at only monetary indicators, it equally covers both health and education[23].

The HDI has replaced the "UNDP" Index for human poverty that measured the population below the poverty line, the availability of water, the proportion of children aged less than 5 years suffering from malnutrition and the probability of death occurring before 40 years of age (UNDP, 2008). Together, these indicators have been useful in fostering better ideas on social development (Dobers and Halme, 2009).

2.2.2. From Economic Development to Sustainable Development

In order to rise above the polarized vision of the meaning of the word "development", considered either as a means for economic growth or colonial exploitation, it would be wise to adopt a larger point of view integrating many different factors (Dobers and Halme, 2009); consequently, "development" could refer to *"a genuine wish to pass from a life characterized by much suffering and little choice to a life where fundamental needs are satisfied and/or the choices are numerous, and with a viable and responsible utilization of resources"* (Rosling et al., 2006; Sen, 1999).

Sustainable Development (SD), which is defined as *"a development that meets the needs of the present without compromising the capacity of future*

---

[23]UNDP – United Nations Program for Development, 2008

generations to meet their needs" (Brundtland, 1987), fits perfectly with the problematic because it advocates three causes: environmental, social, and economic. Companies that adhere to sustainability therefore seek equilibrium between these three elements. This search for equilibrium should manifest itself by a voluntary yet formalized integration of the three SD elements as part of the strategy of a company (Biwolé et al., 2008; Spence et al., 2007).

Contrary to the strategies of *predatory* multinationals who have sought to transform poor populations into *"homo consumericus"* or into dependant workers, here in this case, it is a matter of establishing ambitious compromises between the viable economic imperatives of the company and different partners by respecting as much as possible their specificities (Martinet and Payaud, 2011). Again, representing the company, should we decide to fully integrate ourselves with the chosen sites and, far from exploiting them, become attached to the land and actually live there ourselves? (Martinet and Payaud, 2011) Finally, must we remind ourselves of the common sense adage: *"no organism can develop or thrive in a setting that is impoverished or in a desert*[24]*"*?

Having such a deep and well-informed knowledge-base, we can now take into consideration the prerequisites for development, such as: potable water and distribution, lodging and other forms of material comfort, health and education services, human rights and gender equality, liberty and democracy, and the equitable distribution of economic growth while taking into account the sustainable use of natural resources. Thus, these basic needs become at the same time an end unto themselves and a means to realize progress (Dobers and Halme, 2009).

Moreover, economic growth for a long-time has been viewed as a *conditio sine qua non* for global development, but many dimensions that are non-economic are today considered as crucial for the viability of the market economy and the lasting survival of human development (Rosling et al., 2006). For example, here is our short list of some important indices: human capital (with an educated and healthy population), public institutions (police, law courts, fiscal administration, legal system, and land registry), and civil society (labor unions, NGO, religious organizations with strong values), and good governance (leadership and government in the best interest of the majority without corruption) (Rosling et al., 2006).

---

[24]Declaration by the President of Danone, Le Monde, 03/03/09

2.2.3. Principles of Sustainable Development (SD)

The SD thus supposes an equilibrium, as harmonious as possible, between the economic, the social, and the environmental aspects (Martinet and Payaud, 2011; Biwolé et al., 2008; Spence et al., 2007; Ernult and Ashta, 2007). Concretely, the SD is also based on three general principles; namely, fairness, precautionary measures, and participation (Ernult and Ashta, 2007).

2.2.3.1. The Principle of Fairness

This principle must be available on three levels:

- In a country, it consists essentially of ensuring that the needs of everyone are met by a better distribution of wealth (poverty reduction).
- Between countries or peoples, it rests on the understanding that the environment is a common and global entity and all must share its resources. The stakes rest notably on the development of developing countries, fair trade, etc.
- Finally, sustainable development supposes fairness that is not only intra-generational (poverty reduction, North-South relations), but also inter-generational (stable climate, preservation of biodiversity, etc.), in other words, both an opening on our spatial horizon (fairness between countries or peoples) and our temporal horizon (fairness between generations).

2.2.3.2. The Principle of Precautionary Measures

This principle consists of foreseeing and preventing unwanted environmental consequences for all projects. It completes the prevention aspect (not to be confused with prudence) when faced with projects that turn out to carry risks. Concretely, it balances the immediate tangible benefits and the future costs, that are difficult to evaluate, potentially high, and often covered up. The preoccupations of *short-termers* generally win over those who take into account long-term perspectives (Ernult and Ashta, 2007). This is why, although the majority of international treaties and agreements regarding the environment mention this principle, they are often difficult to apply (*e.g.*, Both Canada and the United States withdrew from the Kyoto Protocol.).

2.2.3.3. The Principle of Participation

SD is a collective responsibility that requires the active participation and collaboration of all, especially at every level. Consultation and dialogue at all decisional levels (international organizations, States and governments, enterprises, unions, non-governmental organizations, decentralized or local collectives, etc.) are indispensible for sustainable management of resources and, consequently, leads to new modes of governance (Ernult and Ashta, 2007).

In summary, we could say that a better understanding of local realities and mechanisms for development would help in better identifying and orienting the concerted efforts in approaching CSR. The latter therefore presents itself as an answer to local constraints, a means to fill the void left by the authorities, and an alternative path to improve the lives of the population at large.

2.3. CSR in Developing Countries

2.3.1. CSR in Developing Countries: Review of Current State of Affairs

It goes without saying that there is considerably more research on CSR in developed countries than in developing countries *(Dobers and Halme, 2009;* Jamali and Mirshak, 2007; Jamali, 2007; Luken, 2006). The various initiatives in areas of CSR that have been realized in these last few years in the western world have not been accompanied by similar interests or activities with the same zeal in the developing world *(*Jamali, 2007*)*.

Yet, we can confirm that the need for CSR is more pronounced upon review, and that CSR is increasingly recognized by decision makers and international organisms such as the World Bank and the United States Agency for International Development (USAID) as an alternative path, facilitating and accelerating development, particularly in emerging economies (Jamali and Sidani, 2011; Blowfield, 2005; Jenkins, 2005).

Furthermore, to worsen matters, in developing countries there are insufficient social benefits and serious obstacles to proper governance. In other words, the institutions that provide social benefits are generally less prevalent in poorer countries than in wealthier countries. In lieu of these circumstances, companies therefore encounter higher expectations and demands in order to fill these gaps *(Dobers and Halme, 2009;* Baughn et al., 2007). At the very least, they are asked to reduce, even suppress, their negatively viewed outsourcing (Tahari, 2008) that greatly hinders the economic growth of local populations.

Researchers, conscious of the enormous potential of the concept and of its eventual scope, only began in the early years of the 21st century to examine the question and attempt to better understand this new phenomenon in the context of developing countries (Jamali and Mirshak, 2007; Jamali, 2007). Others question the role of local companies (Boutti, 2009; Gherib et al., 2009; M'hamdi and Trid, 2009; Tahari, 2008) as well as the institutional framework favouring, or not, the introduction of socially responsible companies (Labaronne and Gana-Oueslati, 2011).

2.3.2. Philanthropy Stronger Than Strategy

Empirical studies show a certain narrowing regarding CSR when it comes to volunteers and their tasks, along with the economic, judicial, and ethical dimensions that invariably ensue (Jamali and Mirshak, 2007; Jamali, 2007). In fact, when asked on the type of CSR they adopted, companies automatically invoke their philanthropic programs with no mention of ethical considerations, judicial conformity, or economic interventions (Jamali and Mirshak, 2007; Jamali, 2007).

The resulting effect on CSR, within organizations, is to remain compartmentalized in the category of an *"altruistic responsibility"*, according to the typology by Lantos[25] (2001, 2002), who insists that organizations fulfill and acquit themselves of their philanthropic responsibilities without taking into account the financial advantages. Well, the strategic aspect of CSR cannot be so easily dismissed.

Adding value to shares while favouring societal[26] values as well is certainly a desirable scenario for profit-oriented organizations (Jamali, 2007; Porter and Kramer, 2003; Drucker, 1984). This is particularly true in developing countries where a slowdown or work stoppage related to CSR has a tendency to occur often and where serious macroeconomic constraints may force companies to focus solely on their viability and on their return on investment to their shareholders (Jamali, 2007).

Such an approach is very open to criticism. For example, Drucker (1984) emphasized that social responsibility and profitability are not always incompatible and that companies must convert their social responsibilities into commercial opportunities or ventures. As well, Porter and Kramer (2003) suggested a philanthropic approach centered on a context that requires companies to utilize their unique attributes to fulfill social needs in their own corporate context thus favoring a convergence of interests

---

[25]Lantos (2001, 2002) identifies three types of CSR: ethical, altruism and strategic.
[26]"Doing well while doing good" as said by Benjamin Franklin

between companies and society and a reconciliation of social and economic objectives (Porter and Kramer, 2003).

Therefore, instead of *polishing* their image through existing activities to make them more attractive and socially responsible, companies are invited to find what we qualify as "CSR Innovation" (Halme and Laurila, 2009). Concretely, it would mean tackling a social problem (such as a lack of water, food, housing, waste treatment, or financing by micro-credits) as a source for new innovative initiatives *(Dobers and Halme, 2009)*. This new approach already has a following: the housing project for the poor, *Cemex Patrimonio Hoy,* in Latin America, the *Grameen Bank* or *Wizzit* micro-financing in South Africa, and the *Danone* yogurts for children in Bangladesh[27].

It is interesting to see not only companies but also international non-governmental organizations adopt and apply these ideas in their own field of activities *(Dobers and Halme, 2009)*. What comes to mind particularly is the encouragement to take the initiative and reinforcing the entrepreneurial spirit among impoverished peoples rather than simply providing direct assistance (Martinet and Payaud, 2011; *Dobers and Halme,* 2009; Stiglitz and Charlton, 2005).

Taken as a whole, these ideas propose a fundamentally different type of action by which companies can fulfill their responsibilities towards developing countries *(Dobers and Halme, 2009)*.

2.3.3. The Role of Local Companies

Researchers agree on the fact that by following the practices of companies in developed countries, companies in developing countries must first recognize their own responsibilities vis-à-vis their milieu and take conscience of the stakes that CSR presents (Labaronne and Gana-Oueslati, 2011; Boutti, 2009; Gherib et al., 2009; M'hamdi and Trid, 2009; Tahari, 2008). It is true that the results of certain studies undertaken show that local companies are increasingly conscious that social responsibility practices can bring some advantages, but unfortunately CSR remains a concept relatively little known in developing countries (M'hamdi and Trid, 2009).

To remedy this, Labaronne and Gana-Oueslati (2011) suggest that local organizations adhere to the *Global Compact* and conduct *reporting* of SD by using the GRI indicators - *Global Reporting Initiative,* or better still, to

---

[27]For more illustrations, we invite you to consult the site: http://www.scoop.it/t/csr-cases

commit to the necessary steps leading to certification regarding the references and the norms issued by, notably, the *International Standard Organisation* (ISO). All the more so since these organizations are encouraged in their SD initiatives and their social, economic, and environmental responsibilities by international mechanisms (*i.e.* The Sustainable Development Program thanks to the Global Pact financed by the Italian Ministry of Foreign Affairs to profit Moroccan, Tunisian, and Albanian companies).

2.3.3.1. The Global Pact As a Basis for Growth

As we have previously stated, the *Global Compact* advocates the adoption of fundamental values inspired from four major texts (*i.e.*, The Universal Declaration of the Human Rights, The Declaration by the International Labour Organization, The Rio Declaration on the environment and development, and The United Nations Convention against Corruption) that are then presented as ten universal principles (See Table 1) that companies and organizations, in order to adhere to the *Global Compact*, promise to apply.

By acting as such, companies demonstrate their commitment in promoting SD and, indirectly, CSR. It shows as well their willingness to communicate the progress that they realize in their respective fields (Labaronne and Gana-Oueslati, 2011). This undertaking, called "Communicating progress" (COP), requires participants to communicate annually with their stakeholder partners by describing how they are implementing the principles of the *Global Compact* and reporting their results, either anticipated or attained. In order to do this, the form of communication can be submitted as a SD report or any other public report, from a web site, or other means of communication that will ensure that the message is understood.

A company or organization that agrees to such an initiative sends positive signals that lend optimism regarding their degree of immersion in concepts so critical for their country to grasp, CSR and SD. That being said, other authors believe that it would be more reasonable to mitigate the expectations and the requirements that we impose on companies operating in developing countries. These authors remind us, for example, that contrary to developed countries having a solid institutional environment where CSR is synonymous with policies and actions that surpass economic and legal requirements, countries in the developing world will always be subject to the uncertainties that these factors represent because the regulatory framework has not yet been solidly developed and entrenched *(Dobers and Halme, 2009)*.

Jamali and Mirshak (2007) observed that in developing countries, there exists a variety of legal and environmental factors that merit particular attention, if the status of CSR is to be achieved. For them, in a *weak* institutional environment where the non-respect for laws, fiscal evasion, and fraud are the *"norm"* and not the exception, the respect in itself of laws and regulations in force may constitute or be seen as a social responsibility (Jamali and Mirshak, 2007).

Faced with such a concept, in a nation where laws are ignored, these companies are asked to contribute towards improving the detection of fraud, fiscal or otherwise, and join the struggle against unfair competition, and corruption (Jamali and Mirshak, 2007).

2.3.3.2. ISO Certification: A Common Language

Standardization requires points of reference that include technical and commercial solutions, established by experts and professionals in that particular field, regarding the products, goods, and services to be traded (Labaronne and Gana-Oueslati, 2011). These references are published in order to establish a common language for everyone, thus facilitating dialogue between manufacturers, clients, and other partners. Such documents clearly define a common vocabulary, dimensions, characteristics, test samples, various rules, all which facilitate trade. These are the norms, and the best-known standards are unquestionably the "ISO standards".

The International Standards Organization is comprised of 163 members[28] representing the National Standards Institute of member countries of the industrialized world, the developing world, and those countries in transition, of all sizes and regions of the world. Its reason for being is to provide the world economy, governments, and society as a whole the necessary specific tools to address the three sections – economic, environmental, and societal – of SD.

In all its communications, the ISO claims that its standards bring a positive contribution to the world in which we live because it facilitates commerce, favours the sharing of knowledge, and contributes to the dissemination of technological progress, sound practices for management, and evaluation of ISO conformity. The ISO is categorical when it comes to the legitimacy of its works. For it, *"An ISO international standard represents a consensus by the world on the most advanced knowledge concerning that subject matter"*[29]

This organization will soon celebrate its 65 years of existence and the publication of some 20,000 standards. Until the 1980s, its field of competence

---

[28]Source: www.iso.org
[29]www.iso.org/iso/iso_26000_project_overview.pdf (page 2)

was solely concerned with technological subjects. The launch of the ISO 9000 family on the management of quality marked the first expansion in such a field of competency by the ISO towards framing more socio-technical subjects (Helfrich, 2008).

Since 2005, a new step was undertaken with the launch of a new standards project, completely original by its theme, its method of development, structural expertise, and its control methods (Helfrich, 2008). This standard, ISO 26000, published on November 1st 2010, has a clearly defined objective to establish the principle guidelines for developing countries.

According to Labaronne and Gana-Oueslati (2011), there exists an incentive for companies already in developing countries if they want to integrate their procedural approach to both CSR and SD to their strategy; namely, the fact that will not have to start from scratch. They would have the opportunity to rely on tools that already exist, in particular the standards for quality management (ISO 9001), environmental management (ISO 14001, EMAS), work related security management (OHSAS 18001), and eco-design (ISO/TR 14062). These are the same tools that favour the continuous improvement in the global performance of companies. As for harmonizing their performance with their social responsibilities, the ISO 26000 standard would be a good means for control.

2.3.4. ISO Standard 26000: Overview[30]

According to its designers, the ISO 26000 Standard offers principal guidelines regarding societal responsibility, thus providing to organizations of all types, whether from the private sector or the public sector, harmonized guidelines that are pertinent worldwide and based on an international consensus of experts representing the principal groups of stakeholders. Consequently, it encourages the application and the implementation of better practices in social responsibility across the world.

ISO 26000 will create a value added system for existing work on social responsibility (SR), by favouring understanding and by extending the scope of implementation because:

It is linked to creating an international consensus on the direction SR should take and questions, precisely, what organizations must consider:

---

[30]Source: Project ISO 26000: "Tour d'horizon", a presentation brochure of a standard realized by the ISO and available on the site: www.iso.org/iso/iso_26000_project_overview.pdf

✓ It provides guidelines to translate principles into effective actions
✓ It refines the best practices already established and distributes them worldwide for the well-being of the international community.

This standard is applicable to all types of organizations, whether private or public, in developed countries and in the developing world, as well as economies in transition. It will help them in their efforts aimed at operating in a socially responsible fashion which society increasingly demands today. However, it is important to note that the ISO 26000 is a guideline, and not a requirement. Therefore, *it is not intended for certification* as are the standards ISO 9001:2008 and ISO 14001:2004.

ISO 26000 can be invoked to help all types of organizations, regardless of their size, activity, or location in order to operate in a socially responsible manner by providing the proper guidelines for:

✓ The concepts, terms and definitions concerning social responsibility
✓ The context, tendencies, and characteristics of social responsibility
✓ The principles and practices regarding social responsibility
✓ The questions and fundamentals regarding social responsibility
✓ The integration, realization and promotion of responsible behaviour throughout organizations, including policies and practices in its sphere of influence
✓ The identification of stakeholder parties and a dialogue with them
✓ The communication of commitments, performances, and other information regarding social responsibility

Published since November 1st, 2010, the ISO 26000 integrates the full international expertise of social responsibility. It provides the questions that an organization must consider in order to operate in a socially responsible fashion and the best practices to apply SR. The ISO 26000 is a powerful SR tool that can help organizations *pass from good intentions to better practices.*

That being said, despite the lofty ambitions and commendable objectives that it aspires to achieve, ISO 26000 already attracts criticism questioning its role despite its recent adoption. Did the authors rush to criticise? Perhaps they did. Nevertheless, we find their arguments plausible; consequently, we have decided to include them in this research paper to ensure objectivity and to prepare for the reader the most complete possible review of the subject matter.

First, they even criticise the theoretical base on which the standard itself is founded. In fact, during the draft phase of the standard, the stakeholder parties were far from reaching a consensus (Helfrich, 2008). The definition of *"stakeholder"* is very dear in the founding works by Freeman (1982) without insisting on the theoretical contributions that followed. Nevertheless, many authors[31] completed the *stakeholder theory*, thus refining the characteristics of the stakeholder parties and their interactions. These complementary details insist on the inequalities of power as well as the differences of involvement or objectivity by these groups of heterogeneous actors, indeed antagonists. Now, this analytical wealth is hardly solicited at all in the ISO standard and it still does not reach consensus (Helfrich, 2008).

The other criticism leans in the direction with the detractors of the very concept of CSR. We have already presented a few. They argue that CSR is, in the final analysis, nothing more than a concept born by occidental hegemony allowing them to impose their supremacy on poor countries; it could even be considered as an ideological movement designed to legitimize and defend the powers of large firms (Devinney, 2009; Banerjee, 2008; Banerjee, 2007). The ISO standards are therefore nothing but additional tools to attain this objective.

In their article *"ISO-lating - Corporate Social Responsibility in the Organizational Context: A Dissenting Interpretation of ISO 26000"*, Birgitta Schwartz and Karina Tilling examine in a critical way the rationality behind the development of standards such as ISO 26000 (Schwartz et al., 2009). They illustrate the fact that by formalising and having standards for social responsibility, the knowledge of local conditions and specificities that is crucial for development is lost, the very same consideration that is crucial for a pertinent CSR development. Normalizing the framework of CSR practices is not an insignificant undertaking for this latter group and it proves to be a potential source of bias. These attempts at standardization invite the same controversy between certain players of CSR who fear that the norm will be reduced to *"an exercise of check marks"* (Commenne et al., 2006) and advance the risk that the management of CSR will become a branch of the *Directorate of Communication and Public Relations* (Allouche et al., 2004).

REFERENCES

Acquier, A., & Aggeri, F. (2007). *The Development of a CSR Industry: Legitimacy and Feasibility as the Two Pillars of the Institutionalization*

---

[31]Helfrich (2008) citing Carroll [1989]; Mitchell & al. [1997]; Hill & Jones [1992]; Semal [2006]; etc

Process. in De Bakker F., den hond F., Neergard P. (eds), Corporate Social Responsibility in Action: Talking Doing and Measuring, Ashgate Publishing, pp. 149-165; 17 pages.

Acquier, A., & Gond, J.-P. (2007). *Aux sources de la responsabilité sociale de l'entreprise : à la (re)découverte d'un ouvrage fondateur.* Social Responsibilities of the Businessman d'Howard Bowen, Finance contrôle Stratégie, Vol. 10, No. 2.

Acquier, A., Gond, J.-P., & Igalens, J. (2005). *Des fondements religieux de la responsabilité sociale de l'entreprise à la responsabilité sociale de l'entreprise comme religion.* Cahiers du Centre de Recherche en Gestion - Université de Toulouse 1, No. 166.

Aggeri, F., Pezet, E., Abrassart, C., & Acquier, A. (2005). *Organiser le développement durable.* Paris, Vuibert; 288 pages.

Aldrich, H. (1979). *Organizations and environments.* Prentice-Hall; 384 pages.

Allouche, J., Huault, I., & Schmidt, G. (2004). *Responsabilité Sociale des Entreprises : la mesure détournée?.* Actes du Congrès de l'AGRH, UQAM, ESG, Montréal.

Astley, W.G., & Fombrun, C.J. (1983). *Collective Strategy: Social Ecology of Organizational Environments.* Academy of Management Review, Vol.8, No. 4.

Banerjee, S.B. (2008). *Corporate Social Responsibility: The Good, the Bad and the Ugly.* Critical Sociology, Vol. 34, No. 1.

Banerjee, S.B. (2007). *Corporate Social Responsibility. The Good, the Bad and the Ugly.* Edward Elgar: Cheltenham; 224 pages.

Baughn, C.C., Bodie, N.L.D., & McIntosh, J.C. (2007). *Corporate Social and Environmental Responsibility in Asian Countries and Other Geographical Regions.* Corporate Social Responsibility and Environmental Management, Vol. 14, No. 4.

Berle A., & Means, G. (1932). *The Modern Corporation and the Private Property.* New York. Mc Millan; 396 pages.

Bertin, A., & Clement, M. (2007). *Pauvreté et économie de pénurie en Union Soviétique : une relecture à partir de l'approche par les culpabilités.* Cahier du Groupe de Recherche en Économie Théorique et Appliquée (GREThA), Université Montesquieu Bordeaux IV (France).

Biwolé, V.O., Spence, M., & Ben Boubaker Gherib, J. (2008). *Stratégies de développement durable dans les PME : Une étude exploratoire auprès des PME camerounaises*, Communication présentée au 9ème CIFEPME, Louvain-la-Neuve (Belgique).

Bjorck, F. (2004). *Institutional Theory: A New Perspective for Research into IS/IT Security in Organisations.* Proceedings of the 37th Annual Hawaii International Conference on System Sciences.

Boele, R., Fabig, H., & Wheeler, D. (2001). *Shell, Nigeria and the Ogoni. A study in unsustainable development: II. Corporate social responsibility and 'stakeholder management' versus a rights-based approach to sustainable development,* Sustainable Development, Vol. 9, No. 3.

Blowfield, M. (2005). *Corporate social responsibility: reinventing the meaning of development?.* International Affairs, Vol. 81, No. 3.

Bouquin, H. (2004). *Le contrôle de gestion.* Presses Universitaires de France, Collection Gestion, 6ème édition, Paris; 508 pages.

Boutti, R. (2009). *L'entreprise marocaine face à des responsabilités sociales et sociétales.* Working Paper, Université Ibn Zohr, Agadir (Maroc).

Bowen, HR. (1953). *Social Responsibilities of the Businessman.* Harper & Brothers, New York; 276 pages.

Branco, M.C., & Rodrigues, L.L. (2007). *Positioning Stakeholder Theory within the Debate on Corporate Social Responsibility.* Electronic Journal of Business Ethics and Organization Studies, Vol. 12, No. 1.

Brown, T.J., & Dacin, P.A. (1997). *The Company and the Product: Corporate Associations and Consumer Product Responses.* Journal of Marketing, Vol. 61, No. 1.

Brundtland, G.H. (1987). *Our Common Future.* Oxford: Oxford University Press; 32 pages.

Burnham, J. (1947). *L'ère des organisateurs.* Calmann-Levy; 313 pages.

Campbell, B. (2008). *L'exploitation minière en Afrique : enjeux de responsabilité et d'imputabilité.* Présentation faite dans le cadre de la conférence : exploitation minière et développement durable en Afrique. (www.ieim.uqam.ca).

Capron, M., & Quairel, F. (2004). *Mythes et réalités de l'entreprise responsable.* Paris, La Découverte; 251 pages.

Cardebat, J.M., & Cassagnard, P. (2009). *La RSE comme couverture du risque de réputation.* Version préliminaire (http://clerse.univ-lille1.fr).

Carroll, A.B. (1999). *Corporate Social Responsibility. Evolution of a Definitional Construct.* Business & Society, Business & Society, Vol. 38, No. 3.

Carroll, A.B. (1991). *The Pyramid of Corporate Social Responsibility: Toward the Moral Management of Organizational Stakeholders.* Business Horizons, Vol. 34, No. 4.

Carroll, A.B. (1979). *A three-dimensional conceptual model of corporate social performance.* Academy of Management Review. Vol. 4, No. 4.

Chandler, A. (1988). *La main visible des managers.* Economica; 635 pages.

Charreaux, G., & Pitol-Belin, J.P. (1987). *Les Théories Des Organisations.* Economica; 35 pages.

Cochoy, F. (2002). *Une petite histoire du client, ou la progressive normalisation du marché et de l'organisation.* Sociologie du Travail, Vol. 44, No. 3.

Commenne, V., Atidegla, A., Champion, E., Gendron, C., Muñoz, I., & Ramaswany, R. (2006). *Responsabilité sociale et environnementale des acteurs économiques. Mode d'emploi pour plus d'éthique et de développement durable.* Paris : Éditions Charles Léopold Mayer; 296 pages.

Dahlsrud, A. (2008). *How Corporate Social Responsibility Is Defined: An Analysis of 37 Definitions.* Corporate Social Responsibility and Environmental Management, Vol. 15, No. 1.

Delbard, O. (2009). *Pour une entreprise responsable : comment concilier profit et développement durable?.* Le Cavalier Bleu; 136 pages.

Demsetz, H. (1967). *Towards a theory of property rights.* American Economic Review; 13 pages.

Devinney, T.M. (2009). *Is the Socially Responsible Corporation a Myth? The Good, the Bad, and the Ugly of Corporate Social Responsibility.* Academy of Management Perspectives, May.

Dohou-Renaud, A., & Berland, N. (2007*). Mesure de la performance globale des entreprises.* Actes du Congrès Annuel de l'Association Francophone de Comptabilité, Poitiers, France, Mai 2007.

Dobers, P., & Halme, M. (2009), Corporate *Social Responsibility and Developing Countries.* Corporate Social Responsibility and Environmental Management, Vol. 16.

Drucker, P.F. (1984). *The new meaning of corporate social responsibility.* California Management Review; Vol.26, No. 2.

Dumoulin, M.C. (2009). *Analyse De Contenu De La Documentation Portant Sur L'eutonie Gerda-Alexander En Lien Avec La Prévention Des Pathologies Chez Les Musiciens.* Mémoire présenté à la Faculté des études supérieures de l'Université Laval, Faculté De Musique.

Duong, Q.L., & Robert-Demontrond, P. (2004). *Evaluation du consentement à payer des consommateurs pour la labellisation sociale, une application empirique.* Institut de Gestion de Rennes - Université de Rennes 1, Centre de Recherche en Economie et Gestion (CREM).

Dupuis, M., Quer-Riclet, L., Bourdon, W., Queinne, Y., & Doganis, C. (2010). *La responsabilité sociale et sociétale des entreprises : un enjeu majeur du 21e siècle.* Terra Nova; 14 pages.

Ernult, J., & Ashta, A. (2007). *Développement durable, responsabilité sociétale de l'entreprise, théorie des parties prenantes : Évolution et perspectives.* Cahiers du CEREN, No. 21.

Epstein, E.M. (2002). *Religion and business – The critical role of religious traditions in management education.* Journal of Business Ethics, 2002-Springer.

Frederick, W. C. (1994). *From CSR1 to CSR2.* Business and Society, Vol.33, No. 2.

Freeman, R.E. (1984). *Strategic Management: A Stakeholder Approach.* Pitman, Boston; 292 pages.

Freeman, R.E. (2010). Strategic *Management: A Stakeholder approach* (Seconde ed.). New York: Cambridge University Press; 292 pages.

Friedman, M. (1970). *The social responsibility of business is to increase its profits.* New York Times Magazine; 7 pages.

Galbraith, J.K. (1958). *The affluent society*; 276 pages.

Geers, F. (2009). *La responsabilité sociétale des entreprises commence chez le consommateur.* InSites Consulting, Communiqué de presse du 24-07-2009.

Gherib, B.B., Spence, M., & Biwole V.O. (2009). *Développement durable et PME dans les pays émergents : entre proactivité opportunisme et compromis.* Revue Internationale PME, Vol. 20, No. 3-4.

Gindis, D. (2008). *Présentation des Théories de la firme.* INSA de Lyon & Université Lyon 2, OT 5A MESO.

Gond, J.P. (2006). *Contribution à l'étude du concept de Performance Sociétale de l'Entreprise. Fondements théoriques, construction sociale, impact économique.* Thèse de doctorat.

Gond, J.P., & Boxenbaum, E. (2004). *Studying the Diffusion of Socially Responsible Investment : Bricolage and Translation across Cultural Contexts.* Working Paper du LIRHE, No. 398.

Gond, J.P., & Mercier, S. (2004). *Les théories des parties prenantes : une synthèse critique de la littérature.* Actes du 15ème congrès annuel de l'AGRH, UQAM, Montréal.

Gray, R.H., Kouchy, R., & Lavers, S. (1995). *Methodological themes: Constructing a research database of social and environmental reporting by UK companies.* Accounting, Auditing and Accountability Journal, Vol. 8, No. 2.

Halme, M., & Laurila, J. (2009). *Philanthropy, Integration or Innovation? Exploring the Financial and Societal Outcomes of Different Types of Corporate Responsibility.* Journal of Business Ethics, Vol. 84.

Hannan, M.T., & Freeman, J. (1977). *The population ecology of organizations.* American Journal of Sociology, Vol. 82, No. 5.

Haurie, A., Bresso, M., & Burgenmeier, B. (1996). *Gestion de l'environnement et entreprise.* Presses polytechniques et universitaires romandes; 280 pages.

Helfrich, V. (2008). *La régulation des pratiques de RSE par les normes : Le cas de la norme ISO 26000 sur la responsabilité sociale.* 5e Congrès de l'ADERSE (aderse.org).

Herrera, A.A., Alcañiz, E.B., Pérez, R.C., & García, I.S. (2011). *Epistemological evolution of corporate social responsibility in management: An empirical analysis of 35 years of research.* African Journal of Business Management, Vol. 5.

Hillman, A.J., & Keim, G.D. (2001). *Shareholder value, stakeholder management, and social issues: What's the bottom line?.* Strategic Management Journal, Vol. 22.

Houle, E. (2012). *La Responsabilité Sociale des Entreprises dans les pays en voie de développement avec des problèmes de gouvernance.* Essai au Centre Universitaire de Formation en Environnement (CUFE), Sherbrooke.

D'Humière, P., & Chauveau, A. (2001). *Les pionniers de l'entreprise responsable.* Éditions d'Organisation; 225 pages.

Jamali, D., & Sidani, R. (2011). *Is CSR Counterproductive In Developing Countries: The Unheard Voices of Change.* Journal of Change Management, Vol. 11, No. 1.

Jamali, D., & Mirshak, R. (2007). Corporate Social Responsibility (CSR): Theory and Practice in a Developing Country Context, Journal of Business Ethics, Vol. 72, Springer 2006.

Jamali, D. (2007). *The Case for Strategic Corporate Social Responsibility in Developing Countries.* Business and Society Review, Vol. 112.

Jenkins, R. (2005). *Globalization, corporate social responsibility and poverty.* International Affairs, Vol. 81, No. 3.

Jensen, M. (2001). *Value Maximization, Stakeholder Theory, and the Corporate Objective Function.* Journal of Applied Corporate Finance, Vol. 14, No. 3.

Jensen, M., & Meckling, W. (1976). *Theory of the firm: managerial behavior, agency costs and ownership structure.* Journal of Financial Economics, Vol. 3, No. 4.

Kornaï, J. (1980). *Economics of Shortage.* North Holland, Amsterdam; 631 pages.

Kornaï, J. (1984). *Socialisme et économie de la pénurie.* Economica, Paris; 587 pages.

Labaronne, D., & Gana-Oueslati, E. (2011). *Analyse comparative Maroc-Tunisie du cadre institutionnel de la RSE dans les PME.* Management & Avenir, No. 43.

Lantos, G.P. (2001). *The boundaries of strategic corporate social responsibility.* Journal of Consumer Marketing, Vol. 18, No. 7.

Lantos, G.P. (2002). *The ethicality of altruistic corporate social responsibility.* Journal of Consumer Marketing, Vol. 19, No. 3.

Lee, M.P. (2008). *A review of the theories of corporate social responsibility: its evolutionary path and the road ahead.* International Journal of Management Reviews, Vol. 10.

Levitt, T. (1958). *The dangers of social responsibility.* Harvard Business Review, Vol. 36, No. 5.

Lindgreen, A., & Swaen, V. (2010). *Corporate Social Responsibility.* International Journal of Management Reviews, Blackwell Publishing Ltd and British Academy of Management.

Luken, R.A. (2006). *Where Is Developing Country Industry in Sustainable Development Planning?.* Sustainable Development, Vol. 14, No. 1.

Martinet, C., & Payaud, M. (2011). *Capacités des pauvres et stratégies RSE-BOP,* EURISTIK.

McWilliams, A., Siegel, M.S., & Wright, P.M. (2005). *Corporate Social Responsibility: Strategic Implications.* Rensselaer Working Papers in Economics, No. 506.

M'hamdi, M., & Trid,S. (2009). *La responsabilité sociale de l'entreprise au Maroc: une étude empirique auprès des petites et moyennes entreprises de la région de Fes Boulemane.* Colloque sur La vulnérabilité des TPE et des PME dans un environnement mondialisé, INRPME, 2009.

Milne, M.J., & Adler, R.W. (1999). *Exploring the reliability of social and environmental disclosures content analysis.* Accounting, Auditing and Accountability Journal, Vol. 12, No. 2.

Mitnick, B. (2000). *Commitment, revelation, and the testaments of belief: The metrics ofmeasurement of corporate social performance.* Business & Society, Vol. 39, No. 4.

Nikos, A. (2004). *The origins of social responsability in ancient Greece*, American College of Greece.

Pasquero, J. (2005). *La responsabilité sociale de l'entreprise comme objet des sciences de la gestion. Un regard historique.* in M.F. Turcotte et A. Salmon (Éds.), Responsabilité sociale et environnementale de l'entreprise, Presses de l'Université du Québec.

Pasquero, J. (2004). *Responsabilités sociales de l'entreprise : Les approches nord-américaines.* in Jacques Igalens (dir.), Tous responsables, Paris, Éditions d'Organisation ; 325 pages

Pasquero, J. (2002). *Les défis de la gestion responsable*, in Michel Kalika (dir.), Les défis du management, Paris, Liaisons, coll. Entreprises et carrières; 413 pages.

Pasquero, J. (1997). B*usiness ethics and national identity in Quebec – Distinctiveness and directions.* Journal of Business Ethics, Springer 1997.

Pestre, F. (2007). *Les relations siège-filiales dans les pratiques de responsabilité sociale : Lafarge et la lutte contre le sida en Afrique.* Published in "XVIe conférence de l'AIMS, Montréal.

Phillips, R., Freeman, R.E., & Wicks, A.C. (2003). *What stakeholder theory is not.* Business Ethics Quarterly, Vol. 13.

Pinkston, T.S., & Carroll, A.B. (1996). *A Retrospective Examination of CSR Orientations: Have They Changed?.* Journal Of Business Ethics, Vol. 15, No. 2.

Poirier, G. (2008). *Notes de cours: Méthodes d'analyse qualitative en sciences sociales.* Département d'anthropologie, Faculté des sciences sociales, Université Laval.

Porter, M., & Kramer, M. (2006). *The link between competitive advantage and corporate social responsibility.* Harvard Business Review, December 2006.

Porter, M., & Kramer, M. (2003). *The competitive advantage of corporate philanthropy.* Harvard Business Review on Corporate Social Responsibility, Boston: Harvard Business School Press, December 2002.

Reynaud, E., & Papillon, J.-C. (2003). *Quand l'environnement devient stratégique.* Economies et sociétés (Paris); 289 pages.

Robert-Demontrond, P., & Joyeau, A. (2010). *Résistances des consommateurs à la labellisation sociale : de la critique des modalités à la critique de la logique économique sous-jacente.* 9th International Congress Marketing Trends, Venise (Italie).

Rodić, I. (2007). *Responsabilité sociale des entreprises – le développement d'un cadre européen*. Institut Europeen De L'universite De Geneve; 102 pages.

Rosling, H., Lindstrand, A., Bergström, S., Rubenson, B., & Stenson, B. (2006). *Global Health An introductory textbook*. Studentlitteratur: Lund, WCED - World Commission on Environment and Developmen; 324 pages.

Ross, A. (1973). The economic theory of agency : the principal problem, American Economic Review, LXII, Vol. 63.

Rowley, T., & Berman, S. (2000). A *Brand New Brand of Corporate Social Performance*. Business and Society, Vol. 39.

Schwartz, B., & Tilling, K. (2009). *"ISO-Lating" Corporate Social Responsibility in the Organizational Context: A Dissenting Interpretation of ISO 26000*. Corporate Social Responsibility and Environmental Management, Vol. 16, No. 5.

Scott, W.R. (2001). *Institutions and Organizations*. Thousand Oaks, CA, Sage; 255 pages.

Scott, W.R. (2004). *Institutional theory*. in Encyclopedia of Social Theory, George Ritzer, ed. Thousand Oaks, CA: Sage.

Segal, J.-P. (2003). *La RSE et les conditions de travail*. European Foundation, Dublin

Sen, S., Bhattacharya, C.B., & Korschun, D. (2006). *The Role of Corporate Social Responsibility in Strengthening Multiple Stakeholder Relationships: A Field Experiment*, Journal of the Academy of Marketing Science, Vol. 34, No. 2.

Sen, A. (1999). *Development as Freedom*. Oxford University Press: Oxford; 366 pages.

Solomon, R.C. (1994). *The New World of Business: Ethics and Free Enterprise in the Global 1990s*. Lanham, MD: Rowman & Littlefield Publishers Inc.; 337 pages.

Spence, M., Ben Boubaker Gherib, J., & Biwolé, V.O. (2007). *Une étude exploratoire des fondements du degré d'engagement des PME dans le développement durable*. Journées scientifiques de l'entrepreneuriat de l'AUF, Antananarivo, Madagascar.

Sternberg, E. (1997). *The Defects of Stakeholder Theory*. Corporate Governance, Vol. 5, No. 1.

Stiglitz, J. (2006). *Un autre monde : Contre le fanatisme du marché*. Fayard; 563 pages.

Stiglitz, J., & Charlton, A. (2005). *Fair Trade for All: How Trade Can Promote Development*. Oxford University Press: Oxford; 352 pages.

Sweeney, L., & Coughlan, J. (2008). *Do different industries report corporate social responsibility differently?An investigation through the lens of stakeholder theory*. Journal of Marketing Communications, Vol. 14.

Tahari, K. (2008). *La responsabilité sociale de l'entreprise en économie de transition*. Travail de recherche à l'université d'Oran-Algérie.

Thompson, D. (2003). *Tools for Environmental Management: A Practical Introduction and Guide*. University of Calgary, Departmentt of Archaelogy; 452 pages.

Tsoutsoura, M. (2004). *Corporate Social Responsibility and Financial Performance, Applied Financial Project*. Haas School of Business, University of California at Berkeley.

Vlachos, P.A., & Tsamakos, A. (2011). *Corporate social responsibility: Attributions, loyalty and the mediating role of trust*, Journal of the Academy of Marketing Science, Vol. 37, No. 2.

Waddock, S., & Graves, S. (1997). *The corporate social performance – financial performance link*. Strategic Management Journal, Vol. 18.

Wernerfelt, B. (1995). *The Resource-Based View of the Firm: Ten Years After*. Strategic Management Journal, Vol. 16, No. 3.

Wernerfelt, B. (1984). *A Resource-based view of the firm'*, Strategic Management Journal, Vol. 5.

Windsor, D. (2001). *The future of corporate social responsibility*. The International Journal of Organizational Analysis, Vol. 9, No. 3.

Wood, D.J. (1991). *Corporate Social Performance Revisited*. Academy of Management Review, Vol. 16, No. 4.

In: Multinational's CSR Practices …
Editor: Alidou Ouedraogo

Chapter 1

A PLEA FOR A CHINESE MODEL OF ETHICAL LEADERSHIP

A. Barraquier

SKEMA Business School, France

INTRODUCTION

Tourists, business people or scholars visiting China are intrigued when reading a Chinese newspaper or watching Chinese television channels, about the obsession of China to become the leading economic power. This obsession probably reflects the aspiration of the Chinese population as a whole, the strong patriotic spirit that exists in China, and the desire to be recognized as the world leading dominant power. The idea of the competition with the US is prevalent.

However, being an economic giant is not enough to establish leadership, because leadership is not only about power and economic supremacy. As argued by the different theories of leadership (trait, behavioral, contingent or emotional intelligence theories), it is also about values, in particular, those of integrity, respect, care and virtue, four Confucianist values which have guided China throughout its long history. For many of them, Chinese corporations do not, unfortunately, display these values. Corruption, unprotected labor, toxic products, environmental crime is reported daily in the Chinese press. Can we expect that Chinese corporations change their practices and if they do, can they contribute to impose Chinese multinationals as respected leaders? In this chapter I'm exploring that issue, and make suggestions for these corporations to become true ethical leaders.

INTRODUCTION: WITH GREAT POWER COMES GREAT RESPONSIBILITY

Chinese corporations are prone (and perceived) to become the largest, the most numerous, and possibly the most influential organizations in the world. As citizens of the world will learn to identify them, they will be regarded as powerful players, and will be expected to act as such. "With great power comes great responsibility," wrote the French philosopher Voltaire.

China's emerging economy represents 8 trillion US dollars, a big share of today's global economy, and about half the size of the US economy. Over the past few years, it has left behind each of the significant economies in Europe, one by one, is now considered to be the second largest economy and is expected to get ahead of the US around 2020, if not before that. Such an achievement means a lot to Chinese people, who have been waiting a long time to be recognized as a great nation. Europeans tend to forget, or simply ignore, the humiliation that European powers have inflicted to China and its people, during the 19th century. France, Germany, England and Russia imposed semi-colonialism and the trade and circulation of opium (after the two opium wars) to China. In a famous episode, the French and the British troops invaded and destroyed Yuanmingyuan, known as the Old Summer Palace today. Visitors who visit the ruins of the palace in northern Beijing are reminded of the brutality of the assailants. This episode was followed by a series of treaties imposed to China, known as the "unfair treaties." Knowing that period of Chinese history can help understand the national sentiment that exists in China today. Moreover, when China reopened its doors to foreign powers at the end of the seventies, the arrogance and sense of superiority of Western firms during the golden era of joint ventures with Chinese partners, contributed to rekindle old sentiments of defiance.

The time has come for China. It has demonstrated its capacity to be an influential power, through a spectacular economic transformation. Yet, becoming the world's largest economy might not be enough to be regarded as a leader. China must undertake significant action to send positive signals about social and environmental concerns, a threat for its economic supremacy. If not, its supremacy will only confer China a domination status instead of the leadership status expected from a powerful nation. In that enterprise, Chinese corporations have a significant role to play: they hold responsibility in most of the severe environmental and health crises that occurred in the past few years. In the 21st century, public and private organizations exert influence and power beyond the economic sphere, because citizens voice their concerns regarding a broad range of ethical, social and environmental issues.

The theories of leadership have put an emphasis on the various aspects that enable the emergence of leadership capabilities. At the individual level, leadership is related to personality and charisma, but at a more general level, it refers to the capacity to impose a vision, to drive and support the motivation of followers. It is also connected to the intellectual and emotional qualities that drive people to respect and admire leaders. At the corporate level, firms considered to be leaders in their field must ensure that their reputation is high among their stakeholders to keep their positions as leaders. The attributes of reputation that strengthen leaders are diverse. They encompass creativity, the capacity to innovate, the financial solidity of the firm, corporate history, and last but not least, the responsibility and ethical behavior of organizations.

Soft power plays a tremendous role in leadership positions. American corporations have contributed, after the Second World War, to the dissemination of the American dream: entrepreneurial success, the American way of life and the abandonment of rigid social codes inherited from the old European democracies, have appealed to millions of people from all cultures, with no exception. In Europe, although European nations stepped down from the dominant positions they occupied prior to the war, the European culture remains attractive to many people throughout the world. A number of organizations greatly contributed to this long-lasting model. For instance, the undisputable domination of Italian and French firms in the fashion and luxury industry is grounded on the 'art de vivre', a combination of esthetics and well-being.

Nevertheless, most people view the U.S model as prevalent, being the most powerful and the most influential. It is probably why China regards the U.S as a model to surpass, but also as a cultural model to imitate. The problem is that the U.S model is not only losing momentum, but also being questioned. The recent financial crisis has shown the limits of a capitalist model that creates increasing inequalities and uncertainties than jobs and prosperity for the majority. The consumption model is highly criticized and weakens the foundations of American society as much as other societies elsewhere, who have adopted a liberal economy.

The world might be looking for another model of leadership, not for a capitalist model that triggers growing concern around the globe.

ANCHORING CSR IN CULTURAL CONTEXTS

Corporate social responsibility (CSR) has emerged as a concept in the U.S management literature in the fifties, and became popular in American corporations in the decades that followed. It has only recently picked up at the international level. Twenty years ago, the general public in China, France or Brazil had very little or no knowledge of what CSR was about, a situation that has now totally changed with the development of CSR initiatives all over the world.

CSR Different Backgrounds

Corporate philanthropy was preexisting to the concept of CSR in many countries around the world. The idea of wealthy merchants contributing to charitable activities organized, in particular, by religious institutions, has been pervasive in ancient cultures in Asia, the Middle East, or Europe in the past hundreds of years and in the new world nations such as Latin and North America or Australia in the twentieth century.

In its most recent forms, social responsibility tends to be drawing from traditional values inherited from religious, philosophical, historical, social and economic contexts characterizing national cultures. Besides, CSR is essentially based on responsiveness to the expectations of salient stakeholders, and across nations, salient stakeholders vary. American corporations tend to focus primarily on shareholders, whereas Japanese companies have historically put an emphasis on customers and European companies on their employees. These patterns are not exclusive in any way, but are explanatory of the role and influence of corporations in given societies.

To illustrate this particular point, let us provide examples. It is striking to observe for instance, that Middle Eastern countries draw extensively from the Islamic principle of the wealthy redistributing to the poor and from the other principle of limiting financial revenues that one can obtain from property or financial speculation, in their conceptions of CSR. In India or Vietnam where extreme poverty is still endemic in spite of the emergence of a rich middle class, CSR policies in private corporations are largely oriented towards policies providing for the poor. In the European Union, where the social model of generalized solidarity organized by a powerful state has been prevalent, the CSR model involves public administrations at the European, national and regional levels, in a private /public partnership perspective. Besides, CSR in Europe focuses enormously on employees as stakeholders; indeed, Europeans tend to look down on shareholders who are highly symbolic of exploitation of labor, a fundamental idea of Marxist theory, whereas in the United States, shareholders have, for decades, represented the American dream of entrepreneurial success. Of course, he financial crisis of 2008 has considerably damaged that representation and there is a vivid debate ongoing in the U.S on the values of capitalism. This debate has crossed borders and the question of reflecting upon new forms of capitalism or alternative models to capitalism is progressing everywhere, including in the political, the economic and the academic spheres[32]. This is precisely why the willingness of China, Chinese people and Chinese entrepreneurs to copy the U.S model of capitalism as it is, appears profoundly disturbing to many observers.

Even though China defends its model as being different, in particular because of the central role that the Chinese government plays in the Chinese economy, there is no ambiguity upon the direction that the country is taking with its economic reforms, but also with the transformation of values. Encouragements to become rich and successful are both tacit and explicit, since for instance, Chinese television channels depict the capitalist successes of Chinese entrepreneurs with obvious signals of envy and admiration (tacit recognition), and since property laws have been deregulated to such an extent that wealthy individuals have no limit to their fantasy homes, such as cheap reproductions of royal castles from old Europe.

This triggers interesting questions specific to the Chinese context and experience. If we examine the extent to which the CSR discourse in Chinese corporations draws from traditional values and culture regardless of the tensions created by the socio-economic context, then we are not surprised at the alarming social, ethical and environmental situation that Chinese people confront in their daily life, either as consumers, employees or citizens.

To play a more significant role in the Chinese society, and in the betterment of living conditions of people, Chinese corporations should address more strongly the following questions:

---

[32] For instance, the theme of the Academy of Management in 2013 was 'Capitalism in question'. The Academy of Management is the largest management research community and encompasses more than 10,000 members throughout the world.

- How much are the Chinese entrepreneurs interested to promote social and ethical values in their companies? And how important is business ethics, responsibility and sustainability to them?
- How important is it to Chinese leaders and managers to provide safe, enjoyable and caring environments for their employees?
- What is the idea of ethics, responsibility and sustainability for Chinese leaders in general? How relevant do they think it is to business, economics and the country?

If corporations in China do not work diligently on these issues, they will contribute to increase the risk on their reputation and name, which their stakeholders will disseminate, should any serious social, sanitary, environmental of ethical crisis arise. In 1963, the Stanford Research Institute was already warning corporations that they could cease to exist when they lose the support of their stakeholders.

The second part of this chapter develops a perspective relevant to academics as future paths for research, to practitioners interested in the development of CSR practices in Asia, but also and most of all to Chinese leaders, CEOs and executives curious to reflect upon the significant role that Chinese corporations should, and will have to play in the near future.

RATIONALES FOR A CHINESE MODEL OF ETHICAL LEADERSHIP

The CSR model has been praised and advocated by scholars around the world, but in recent years it has been the target of fierce criticism. In its early years, the CSR movement was intimately tied up to a more responsible behavior of corporations, and less about CSR initiatives designed to respond strategically to stakeholders expectations. The stakeholder theory can be interpreted both in normative and strategic ways. Normative perspectives tend to focus on the social contract that corporations have with society, and remind us that business organizations exist because society is willing to support them. Without society's support, they would be deprived of their license to operate. From that perspective, business should attend to the needs of their stakeholders, including those stakeholders with legitimacy but no power, because they are the primary victims of negative externalities generated by the firm's activities. Conversely, the strategic perspective considers stakeholders as groups putting external pressure on the organization, and with a capacity to damage its reputation. As mentioned earlier, the Stanford Research Institute, a group of scholars working on corporate strategy, defined stakeholders as "those groups without whose support the organization would cease to exist". Corporations have broadly relied upon the strategic perspective of CSR, rendering their CSR policies 'subservient to economic interests', satisfying salient stakeholders and instrumentalizing responsible and sustainable initiatives for their own benefit and financial profit, rather than being concerned with the deontology of a responsible and ethical management of business affairs. This critical view is put forward by Western scholars who illustrate it with various examples of American, Canadian or European MNCs.

International Visibility and Reputation of Chinese Corporations

An important characteristic of large Chinese corporations is that they rank third behind the U.S and Japan with 115 billion dollars of outbound investments. Yet, this reality does not correlate with their visibility. If consumers across the world had to name a Chinese brand, they might come up with Lenovo, the computer manufacturer, and maybe a couple of others such as Huawei or Hai'er. These brandnames and the corporations they stand for are only the tip of the iceberg. Indeed, Chinese multinationals strategies ought to be analyzed domestically and internationally. First, as most people know, China is the leading manufacturer for consumer goods in the world and literally floods markets with billions of goods each year. Yet, these goods bear the brandnames of international designers and manufacturers relocating production in China. Chinese exporters are in a way, massively but anonymously present at a global level. Second, there are quite a number of Chinese companies which brandname and market located exclusively in China. The best examples are probably Baidu, the largest web services company in China, and Renren, one of the leading social media on the internet, both recording millions of registered users, but largely ignored abroad. Other sectors such as banking, agriculture, and the food industry also account major players with very little international notoriety. Finally, another rationale for the lack of visibility of Chinese MNCs is that strong actors in technological business-to-business sectors such as aeronautics, telecommunications, or high-speed trains have only emerged recently and are still unknown to international audiences.

These large but unknown Chinese corporations will certainly see their visibility grow on international markets. The situation is somewhat comparable with the situation of large U.S corporations in the fifties. With a very large domestic market, a great number of American companies were totally unknown from the European markets (their first markets after the Americas) for decades. The international expansion of many of them only started in the eighties and nineties. Chevrolet, a legendary car in the United States has made a timid entrance in Europe only a few years ago. A common strategy for late comers is to buy established brands, and China is also adopting this strategy to set its presence on the international stage. Nevertheless, Chinese brandnames are gradually appearing in international markets. This phenomenon will develop considerably in the coming years, exposing Chinese brands, corporations and reputation far more than it has so far. As a result, the CSR policies of Chinese firms will be substantially more exposed and commented than they are today.

Yet, even though international audiences neither have a clear picture of Chinese corporations doing business abroad nor distinguish them individually, the rise of China as a key player on the international scene is widely known. Perceptions however, differ in rich and emerging economies. They are still very negative in western economies, although recent polls[33] show that China's image and influence is better and wider than it was a few years ago, and that the rise of China as a leading power is not questioned anymore.

The headlines in western newspapers over the past two decades suggest a widespread sentiment of defiance towards China. The Asian giant is clearly perceived in Europe and North America as the main cause of unemployment, justified by the massive relocation of most manufacturing industries to China. This negative perception affected the reputation of the Chinese industry so strongly that the Chinese government organized a large advertising campaign in 2011 featuring ordinary scenes filmed in western countries and focusing on the labels of various products where one could read "made in China with engineers from all over the world", "made in China with software from the Silicon valley", or "made in China with French designers". The final image of the film showed the label "made IN China" fading and being replaced by "made WITH China", a tacit but powerful way of saying 'we cooperate'. The message was also a response to the accusations of poor quality which have impaired the reputation of products imported from China, on the issues of both quality and safety. This reputation is probably unfair to the many Chinese

---

[33] See PEWT report

factories which have made considerable efforts to upgrade the quality standards of their production. Unfortunately, it is regularly reinforced by corporate misconduct resulting in serious injuries or death. In the past two years, Chinese newspapers abundantly commented the horrific story of the infant milk contaminated with melamine, or the railway accident that occurred in Wenzhou with the Chinese-based technology high speed train, two affairs that had far more repercussions in China than abroad. In fact, the strong reactions of the Chinese public to these scandals provide the key argument for "a Chinese model of ethical leadership".

In emerging markets where Chinese investments are significant, the perception of China has turned quite positive globally. In Africa, where China is sourcing and buying natural resources, the overall picture is contrasted. Surveys and reports portray divergent and juxtaposed realities. Global surveys conducted in urban areas are very positive in African countries where Chinese investments and presence is important and visible. An explaining factor is that Chinese corporations, whose main interest is an access to African natural resources, have heavily invested in social projects and infrastructures. Yet, in places where Chinese corporations have set up facilities, results are mixed, due to concrete situations of collaboration that brought Africans and Chinese to work together and the difficulties that multicultural encounters tend to produce. In addition, there is a growing resentment among African communities about the problem of Chinese firms importing their labor force from China to work on their facilities and sites in Africa.

Context of CSR in Chinese Corporations

There is an emerging literature on CSR practices, initiatives and orientations of Chinese corporations. How do they differ from their counterparts in the West and elsewhere? Are they following similar paths, in particular in instrumentalizing CSR strategically?

In China, firms have a very strong relationship with the state, a situation due to several decades of a socialist planned economy. Corporations are eager to preserve a good relationship with the government because it has control over the political, legal, and economic system. The Chinese government is the most salient stakeholder in China for corporations, because it controls a great part of economic and social activities, while the Chinese state is still a shareholder in many corporations. This situation is very different from western countries, where salient stakeholders vary across industries and go from NGOs to consumer associations and regulatory agencies. In China, "CSR becomes an agenda for companies to take care of the social–environmental welfare through philanthropy or short-term activities in exchange of state resources". As a result, MNCs in China (Chinese and foreign) work out their CSR policies in forms of public-private partnerships. In the meantime, being preoccupied with the political relationship they wish to maintain with the government, MNCs are less concerned about tackling ethical and social issues to respond to their most legitimate but less powerful stakeholders, namely their consumers, suppliers or employees.

This governance context is however, propitious to corruption. The Chinese have invented the very idea of bureaucracy. Throughout its history, China developed as a nation and maintained unity thanks to the organization of a very strong network of officials (the mandarins) in charge of decentralized representations of the central government. The succession of dynasties is only the result of a weakening central power benefiting to local warlords. Among them, one eventually emerged and started a new dynasty, sometimes after decades of chaos. The Chinese talked about a "change of mandate" (revolution). The bureaucracy structure remained, but the court officials were replaced. Having good relations with the people in charge, has always been key to the continuation of business. Relationships and social networks, called 'guanxi', refer to the various levels of introduction that individuals have in important organizations. This system has always favoured corrupt practices such as bribery, privileges, and access to key positions, and is an endemic problem in the long Chinese history. The independent agency Transparency International, reports every year on the level of corruption measured in more than 170 countries. Scores range from 0 (highly corrupt) to 100 (very clean), and China scores 39, which signals one of the highest corruption scores among leading economic powers. It is better than Russia (28) and India (36), but worse than Brazil (43), and far from leading powers such as the United States (73), Japan (74) or Germany (79), leadership models that China looks up to.

Corruption and conflict of interest is intimately linked to issues of safety, as in the case of the train accident that occurred in Wenzhou in 2011 leaving 40 people dead and 200 injured. Investigations showed that the lack of safety was linked to poor management practices, lack of control on procedures, and conflicts of interests between the state-owned company and the officials involved. Corruption practices go from bribing regulatory agencies to overlook safety, to allocating resources to political or private interests rather than general interest. Other serious cases of unsafe products have occurred in

China, due to the poor enforcement of control procedures by regulatory authorities.

Finally, China faces an extremely severe environmental crisis[34], which affects individual people and communities in many aspects of their lives. The high levels of pollution of soil, air and water cause severe diseases and illnesses and are highly correlated to premature deaths. The awareness of the Chinese population about environmental protection has grown in the past few years, as peoples' lives are being directly affected by the consequences of the natural environment deterioration. Social unrest due to environmental problems has erupted in different parts of the country, leading the central government to take measures, stop emitting permits for new industrial sites and tackle corruption more seriously. Corruption, again, is largely responsible for the lack of regulation enforcement, and the control of permits.

Rationales for a Substantial Ethical Behavior of Chinese Corporations

Social issues in China are serious, and some situations are worsening. The crucial issues that China confronts are detrimental to the satisfaction of Chinese people with their living conditions, detrimental to the reputation of Chinese products, and detrimental to the image that China projects outside. Before China started its irresistible ascension towards economic prosperity, it was common to hear ordinary Chinese people say that they were "eating bitter" (chiku), meaning that they found their life to be hard and their journey through life to be a suffering one. Today, the economic growth has alleviated poverty and allowed hundreds of millions to make a better living. However, inequalities still prevail and become unbearable for the poorest part of the population (*i.e.* the Gini index which measures inequality).

The rationales for corporations to display more ethical behavior are plenty. Most of them are well known and clearly identified by both business communities and the Chinese government. Nevertheless, neither shows a strong commitment towards ethical engagement despite Hu Jintao's 2007 political mandate to strive for a 'Harmonious Society' and implement CSR policies in business firms. Indeed, the Chinese media is filled with daily reports of consumers suing companies because of corporate irresponsibility,

---

[34] For a deeper insight on environmental issues in China, see the remarkable analyses published by the Eurasia Institute of HEC Business School, Paris. These reports are available both in English and French.

and consumers' frustration and anger can only grow in the future. Environmental concerns are rising, and the situation deteriorates, driving populations to demonstrate, overcoming the fear of repression that had been prevalent in the past (the population still remembers the terrible repression of the June 4th demonstrations in 1989). Scandals of corruption also make the headlines, driving ordinary citizens to rebel. In China, people work hard to get out of poverty, and do not benefit any longer from the strong support of the state. Education and health which used to be free for all have become expensive, and out of reach for many. Thus, ethical behaviour and conduct is a necessity to defuse the growing anger taking place in China, and is the 'number one' rationale for Chinese corporations to consider ethical conduct as a major leadership criterion.

The negative image of China relative to the reliability of its products and technology would constitute a second rationale for a drastic move towards ethical behaviour. In China and abroad, Japanese, German and U.S technology and products are incredibly popular because of their quality and reliability, and because of the good reputation of the corporations that manufacture them. The first reaction from Chinese consumers when the poisonous infant milk affair erupted was to turn to western products for their safety. It is also striking to see, that even though the Sino-Japanese relationship is not very good, and that all the surveys conducted in China about Japan show strong dislike and defiance, Chinese consumers continue to buy Japanese products[35]. In fact, they do so because of the unquestionable leadership of Japan on the quality, reliability and safety of their technologies. Japanese corporations have played a tremendous role in maintaining Japanese leadership when Japan could not fully express a political leadership, a condition inherited from its defeat in WW2. In Europe, the situation of Germany is similar.

There is therefore an important challenge for Chinese corporations to adopt a substantial ethical behaviour on core issues, tackling "core responsibilities", instead of displaying symbolic actions of CSR. Besides, Chinese firms end up mimicking western corporations policies, while such policies are under a fire of fierce criticism in rich countries, because they are more symbolic than substantial, driving firms into a state of amoralization. A very strong ethical behaviour can drive China to be noticed as remarkable, and to gradually become an ethical leader.

---

[35] Japanese companies suffer from occasional boycotts from Chinese consumers when the media report about political tensions between the two countries. These tensions arise from unsettled disputes between China and Japan (*i.e.* the recognition by the Japanese authorities of mass killing in China during WW2 in Japanese history books).

Yet, China has to find its own model of leadership, because it has no other alternative to be consistent and to gain credit from the Chinese population, and also because the rest of the world would be interested to see China emerge as an alternative political power not only based on economic performance, but also on social and ethical values. There is a diversity of options that Chinese corporations could be looking at to set up a model of leadership that could attract attention from the international community.

For instance, a promising path could be for Chinese corporations to propose a differentiated governance model that could reflect the much promoted idea of state capitalism, and infuse it with meaning that resonates with individuals and the society, in China and elsewhere. Chinese leaders have argued in the recent past that the Chinese model of capitalism was a superior alternative to traditional capitalism prevailing in western democracies. Yet, inequalities in Chinese society are greater than in democratic societies; the Gini index, which measures revenues inequality by country, observes a deteriorating situation in China over the recent years. This is largely due to high levels of corruption at the provincial and state level, collusion of interests between business and government elites, and a weak legal system leading to a deficiency of social justice. Chinese corporations could play a determining role in shaping governance mechanisms, a redistribution model and a model of stakeholder dialogue which could serve as landmark references for developing and emerging markets corporations.

To sustain the legitimacy of a Chinese leadership in that domain, China has the capacity to draw from its philosophical heritage. The popularity of traditional Chinese philosophy, and the respect that people across the world show for the high ethical and intellectual standards that thinkers such as Confucius, Mengzi, and Laozi have established, should not be taken for granted or as old-fashioned in China, but on the contrary, revived. Their teachings should be much more pervasive in the course curriculum of Chinese business schools. In western countries, European philosophers are discussed in the classroom, and their vision is still popular and widespread in European societies. It allows students to ground their understanding of ethics in their own culture. Courses on business ethics take into account the philosophical and religious traditions, and then examine practice-oriented applications for CSR and sustainable development. Conversely, I have noticed in numerous occasions that my Chinese students undervalued the great insights of their own culture to refer to western references in their attempts to fit in. Chinese civilization is incredibly deep and rich. From the historic annals of Simaqian, to the modern writers like Lu Xun and Bajin, Chinese culture holds untapped reservoirs of knowledge and wisdom. The world, and the western countries in particular, is eager to find new sources of inspiration to regenerate the economic and social models and a framework that would work better for business and society. Without that perspective, and the willingness of Chinese leaders to integrate ethical, responsible and sustainable values in their vision of leadership, China will never be the leader that its people hope for nor the leading power that the world needs.

REFERENCES

Bondy, K., Moon, J. & Matten, D. (2012). An institution of corporate social responsibility (CSR) in multi-national corporations (MNCs) : form and implications. *Journal of Business Ethics, 111,* 2, 281-299.

Bowen, H.R. (1953). *Social responsibilities of the businessman.* Eds: Harper & Brothers.

Bu, Q. (2012). *China's New Approach to CSR in Congo: Is The Leverage Turning to China?* Available at SSRN 2056955.

Commission of the European Communities (2001). *Green paper: Promoting a European framework on CSR.* Available at: http://eur-lex.europa.eu/LexUriServ/LexUriServ.do?uri=COM:2001:0366:FIN:EN:PDF

Callahan, W. A. (2004). National insecurities: Humiliation, salvation, and Chinese nationalism. Alternatives: Global, Local, *Political, 29,* 2, 199-218.

Chan, E. Y. Y., Griffiths, S. M. & Chan, C. W. (2008). Public-health risks of melamine in milk products. *The Lancet, 372,* 9648, 1444-1445.

Chan, A. (2001). *China's workers under assault: the exploitation of labor in a globalizing economy.* ME Sharpe.

Chao, G. L. (2013). *Elite Status in the People's Republic of China: Its formation and maintenance.* Doctoral dissertation, Columbia University.

Cheung, Y. L., Jiang, K. & Tan, W. (2012). 'Doing-good'and 'doing-well'in Chinese publicly listed firms. *China Economic Review, 23,* 4, 776-785.

Donaldson, T. & Dunfee, T. (1994). Toward an unifed conception of business ethics: integrative social contracts theory. *Academy of Management Review, 19,* 2, 252-284.

Freeman, R. E. (2010). *Strategic management: A stakeholder approach.* Cambridge University Press.

Grenié, M. & Belotel-Grenié, A. (2006). *L'éducation en Chine à l'ère des réformes. Transcontinentales*. Sociétés, idéologies, système mondial, *3*, 67-85.

He, W. (2012). *In the Name of Justice: Striving for the Rule of Law in China.* Brookings Institution Press.

Mitchell, R. K., Agle, B. R. & Wood, D. J. (1997). Toward a theory of stakeholder identification and salience: Defining the principle of who and what really counts. *Academy of management review*, *22*, 4, 853-886.

PEWT Research Centre report. (2013). *America's global image remains more positive than China's*. Available at: http://www.pewglobal.org.

Redding, G. (2002). The capitalist business system of China and its rationale. *Asia Pacific Journal of Management*, 2-3, 221-249.

Sauvant, K. (2011). China: Inward and Outward Foreign Direct Investment. *Transnational Corporations Review*, *3*, 1, 1-3.

See, G. K. H. (2009). Harmonious society and Chinese CSR: Is there really a link?. *Journal of business ethics*, *89*, 1, 1-22.

Tsang, M. C. (1994). Costs of education in China: Issues of resource mobilization, equality, equity and efficiency. *Education Economics*, *2*, 3, 287-312.

Wang, H., Yip, W., Zhang, L., Wang, L. & Hsiao, W. (2005). Community-based health insurance in poor rural China: the distribution of net benefits. *Health Policy and Planning*, *20*, 6, 366-374.

Wong, F. F. (1980). *Education and Work in China*. Change, *12*, 8, 24-31.

Wong, K. C. (2001). Chinese culture and leadership. *International Journal of Leadership in Education*, *4(4)*, 309-319.

Zhao, M. (2012). CSR-based political legitimacy strategy: Managing the state by doing good in China and Russia. *Journal of business ethics*, *111*, 4, 439-4.

In: Multinational's CSR Practices ...   ISBN: 978-1-63463-479-3
Editor: Alidou Ouedraogo   © 2015 Nova Science Publishers, Inc.

Chapter 2

CASE STUDY: RENAULT PLANT IN TANGIERS (MOROCCO)[36]

Alidou Ouedraogo

University of Moncton, Canada

INTRODUCTION

Presentation of Renault as a "Responsible Economic Player"

The Renault group of companies is a French automobile manufacturer connected to the Japanese manufacturer Nissan since 1999. This group maintains plants and subsidiaries across the globe. Founded by three brothers Louis, Marcel, and Fernand Renault in 1899, it quickly distinguished itself through innovations. It was nationalized at the end of the Second World War. Considered a "social display" of the country, it was privatised in the 1990s. It promotes automobile racing to promote its own products and is diversified in a number of sectors.

Present on all continents with more than 350 industrial and commercial sites in 118 countries, Renault designs, manufactures, and sells a large variety of innovative vehicles, while confident and respectful of the environment. Today, Renault continues its strategy of profitable growth with its related brands Dacia and Renault Samsung Motors. Renault employs 121 000

---

[36] Thanks Youssef Benghazouani for your collaboration

associates, generated a turnover of $42,628 million euro's in 2011, with a net result of $2,139 million euro's, and sold more than 2.7 million vehicles.

For detailed corporate information on this company, we suggest that the reader consult the document "ATLAS RENAULT - ÉDITION MARS 2011" which provides all the pertinent information regarding this group[37].

RENAULT AS A "RESPONSIBLE PARTNER"

The general management team responsible for corporate social responsibility (GMCSR) is accountable for preparing CSR policy and handling the corporate sponsorship for the group, as well as ensuring its implementation, and initiating innovative and coherent actions in line with the following four priorities of CSR policy: **Education** and **Diversity** in order to promote equal opportunity; **Access to sustainable mobility** for all; and awareness and promotion of sound practices to efficiently counter **highway insecurity.**

The objective of the Renault Group regarding CSR is to limit the impact of their activities by anticipating and then by applying the most stringent international standards (references GRI and ISO 26000) and to implement voluntary initiatives to meet the high expectations of society, notably in its construction basins or area sites.

Renault takes into account the overall impact of its vehicles at each step in the life cycle: design/manufacturing, end usage on roads, and recycling. The objective of this global approach to "life cycle" is to ensure that the automobile leaves less and less of an environmental footprint.

MANUFACTURING

Respect for the environment begins at the production sites. A commitment made by Renault since 1995 has proven to be a complete success: 100 % of production sites at Renault have obtained the environmental certification ISO 14001.

---

[37] Available on the website: www.media.renault.com/documents/InformationKits/Renault_Atlas_ mars_2011.pdf

ISO 14001 Is a Standard That Favours the Environment

It certifies the quality of the environmental management system of the site. In such an industry, it confirms the progress realized, notably, in water and energy utilization / conservation, noise and visual pollution, atmospheric emissions and waste products due to production sites. The certification of all the Renault production sites attests to the willingness of the Group, on a daily basis, to reduce the impact of its activity on the natural environment.

More Than 10 Years of ISO 14001

The Sandouville plant was the first in the group to be certified as ISO 14001 in 1998. The certification cycle continues today by integrating progressively the new industrial facilities by Renault in its worldwide operations (Morocco, India, Russia, etc.). The Group thus reaffirms its willingness to participate at the environmental, economic, and social levels at each of its facilities.

Substantial Progress

Since 1997, the environmental management of industrial sites has allowed for a *reduction* in:

- 30 % energy consumption per vehicle manufactured (Mw/H PCI),
- 65 % water consumption (m3/ vehicle), the equivalent of 5,000 Olympic size swimming pools,
- 70 % of material waste (kg/vehicle),
- 40 % of volatile organic compounds (kg/vehicle),
- 47 % of toxic waste in aquatic basins

Technological Breakthroughs

The experience acquired since 1995 by progressively implementing new technologies in different fields at Renault plants onsite has allowed them to integrate upstream innovative solutions for new industrial sites. Two examples are given:

1) Tangiers, first in the 5th edition of the "Sustainable Energy European awards 2011" organized by the European Union in the category of "production". The Tangiers site is the first facility in the world with a production capacity of 400,000 vehicles per year at 98% carbon-free, due to electricity generated by a wind turbine park and with heating produced by biomass.

2) Sites in France: In partnership with Gestamp Solar, Renault launched the largest solar energy project for automobile manufacturing in the world by installing solar panels in its plants in France. The project involves the sites at Douai, Maubeuge, Flins, Batilly, Sandouville and Cléon (certified ISO 14001 since 2000). The panels will cover a total area of 450,000 m² (equivalent to more than 60 soccer fields) producing 60 MW of power, the annual consumption of a town of 15,000 inhabitants.

FUEL CONSUMPTION

Renault made important strategic choices in favour of the environment. Notably, it was determined to significantly reduce greenhouse gas emissions responsible for global warming. This policy leads directly to the development of a mosaic of technological solutions reachable to all.

Fewer Emissions of CO_2

The signature of the Renault eco² program in May 2007 (Renault eco² vehicles fulfill three ecological criteria in terms of production, CO_2 emissions and recycling) supports this commitment by proposing an economic sub-group of vehicles that consume less than 5.3 l/100 km in diesel fuel, which is less than the 5.9 l/100 km of fuel currently the norm. A number of Renault brand vehicles operate with bio-fuels (E85, B30). These allow for a reduction in CO_2 emissions between 20% and 70%, depending on the bio-fuel used.

The Group is also committed to develop vehicles that function with natural gas and LPG (Liquified Petroleum Gases). Finally, the "zero-emission" target announced by the Renault-Nissan Alliance lends itself to selling a fleet of electric vehicles by 2011.

Consume Less

Less CO2 also equals fewer liters of fuel consumed. By working on better fuel injection, reducing friction, and lightweight materials, the engineers at Renault have concentrated on offering performance-oriented vehicles at reduced fuel consumptions.

Renault is also studying *downsizing*. This technology allows for a reduction in motor cylinder, a result of a turbo compression, while preserving performance. The TCe 100 motor coupled with a 1.6, the power of a 1.4, and the cylinder capacity of 1.2. With such a motor, Renault produces 30% less in fuel consumption compared to the Clio first generation model.

End of Life Cycle
From its initial design, the environmental consequences at the end of the vehicle life cycle are taken into account.

Recycled Plastic
Renault is developing with its suppliers, from the initial design stage, vehicles that have at least 7% recycled plastic overall (Renault eco² fleet). This percentage may even reach 17% on certain models.

Vehicles Recyclable to 85 %
Vehicles from the Renault eco² fleet are recyclable up to 85% at the end of their life cycle. Accordingly, cleaned, dismantled, and crushed, they have a second life. Their recycling allows the generation of electricity (cement plants, heating, etc.) and to create new materials, including recycled plastic.

Renault Environment
In 2008, Renault went one-step further by creating a new subsidiary; namely, Renault Environment. Its mission: to promote the value of products at the end of life cycle and develop new services related to the environment.

Using 95% of Vehicle Mass at End of Life Cycle
As part of the scope of the European project **LIFE +**[38], Renault aims, with project **ICARRE 95** (Innovative CAR REcycling 95%), to demonstrate the

---

[38] Rule (CE) n ° 614/2007 of the "Parlement européen et du Conseil" on May 23 2007 concerning the financial incentive for the environment (LIFE+).
    The program LIFE+ finances projects that contribute to the development and the implementation of the policies and law on matters of the environment. The program

usefulness of 95% of the mass of its fleet of vehicles no longer in use. To attain this objective, Renault is implementing, by associating itself with four industrial partners, a shortened timeframe to reuse residual parts and material.

The Electric Vehicle, a Global Strategy

Renault desires to be the first general vehicle manufacturer to offer zero-emission vehicles accessible to the people at large. The electric vehicle does not emit any CO_2 emissions when on the road. The Renault-Nissan Alliance is developing a complete fleet of 100% electric powered propulsion units whose power will oscillate between 15 kW and 100 kW (20 hp and 140 hp).

For Renault, the electric vehicle represents the real answer and crowning achievement to the current problematic directly linked to the environment and the noise pollution in the cities. Modern technical innovations now allow for the realization of an electric vehicle available to the masses at reasonable costs. In addition, the evolution of vehicle usage makes the electric vehicle ideal for the majority of daily commutes. In 2011, Renault proposes to its clients a complete range of electric vehicles: a utilitarian Kangoo Z.E., the family sedan Fluence Z.E, a new type of urban vehicle for two occupants, the Twizy.... After 2012, the range of electric vehicles will continue to expand to all branches of the industry. To complement these models, Renault will propose innovative services to facilitate their usage as well as advanced batteries currently in the design stage by the Renault-Nissan Alliance.

RENAULT AS A "RESPONSIBLE ECONOMIC PLAYER" IN MOROCCO: AN INTEGRATED AND HOLISTIC APPROACH

Tangiers Plant: A Pilot Industrial Facility

Thanks to a partnership between the Kingdom of Morocco[39], Renault, and Veolia Environment, the plant at Tangiers, opened in February 2012, is both a

---

facilitates, notably, the integration of environmental issues and, more generally, participate in durable development. The program LIFE+ replaces a number of financial instruments dedicated to the environment, such as LIFE that preceded it.

[39] We have included a full presentation on the country entitled: Morocco, a short summary (File 5), taken from the site "Agence Marocaine de Développement des Investissements": www.invest.gov.ma

zero-emission industrial site and a zero-liquid industrial waste site. Truly, it is an exemplary plant and a model for reducing environmental impacts.

The Renault plant in Tangiers, whose vehicle production will be designed specifically for the B0 Logan platform, will commence activities in 2012 with a production line and an annual production capacity of 170,000 vehicles. Eventually, at its peak, the capacity will surpass 400,000 vehicles per year. The environmental impact stemming from the Renault plant in Tangiers will see reductions in the levels never before seen or achieved for a manufacturing assembly plant.

- CO_2 emissions will be reduced by 98%, approximately 135,000 tons less of CO_2 greenhouse gases per year.
- No industrial process liquids will be pumped, emptied, or emitted in the natural surroundings and the feed water required for industrial processes shall be reduced by 70%.

These results will be obtained due to innovations in the manufacturing process, by using renewable energy, as well as an optimized water management cycle.

In recognition of its laudable efforts and performance, Renault was first in the fifth edition of the "Sustainable Energy European Awards 2011", organized by the European Union in the category "Production".

Zero-Carbon Emission Plant

The CO_2 gashouse emissions of the plant in Tangiers will be reduced by 98%, which corresponds to 135,000 tons of CO_2 per year due to the optimization of energy consumption and the use of renewable energy. The remaining few tons will be compensated either by the purchase of carbon credits, or by the production of renewable energy onsite.

Zero CO_2 thermal energy

First Stage: reducing onsite consumption of thermal energy

Renault and Veolia Environment worked together to reduce the consumption onsite, and Renault reconsidered its painting processes, in particular the cooking phase. The combination of using innovative technologies and better practices in terms of energy recuperation in the painting process, a department that uses 70% of the thermal energy of the plant, resulted in a very significant reduction in energy. Consequently, the need for thermal energy in the Tangiers facility will be reduced by 35%, or more than 40 GWh PCI per year, compared to an equivalent plant with the same production capacity.

Second Stage: producing zero-emission thermal energy

Veolia Environment and Renault together identified a CO2 zero-emitting thermal energy production system. Biomass boilers will provide the superheated water at high pressure necessary for the dryers in the painting process, as well as hot water supplying the heating for other industrial processes, along with the air ventilation system for the plant. The biomass boilers will burn, at the beginning, olive pits grown locally. The remaining combustible will be composed, at first, of eucalyptus wood imported by cargo boats from southern Europe. After four years, the eucalyptus wood will be cultivated and harvested in Morocco.

Electricity Generated from Renewable Resources

Thanks to the development of the renewable energies of Morocco, the "Office National d'Électricité" (ONE) of Morocco will ensure that 100% of the electrical needs of the plant are met from sources such as Aeolian wind power, hydraulics, etc.

Zero-Liquid Industrial Waste

The plant at Tangiers will not emit any industrial waste process liquids while reducing 70% used as feed water for industrial processes when compared to equivalent production plants. These results are due to:

- Optimization of industrial processes so as to reduce the requirements for water and minimizing related waste products;
- Utilizing state of the art technologies designed by Veolia Environment to recycle integrally industrial effluents. A number of treatment processes then transforms the effluents into purified water. The water, tested to meet quality standards for processes, is then re-used for manufacturing vehicles.

In total, the equivalent of 175 Olympic size swimming pools[40] per year of water will not be siphoned from the natural fauna.

---

[40]An Olympic swimming pool = 50 m x 25m x 2m = 2 500 m3

For Jacques Chauvet, leader of the Euro-Med region: "Renault, conscious of the ecological and economical stakes to overcome throughout the world, relies on its two partners and on its industrial expertise to develop, at its Tangiers plant, a major break with the past in terms of the impact of automobile production on the environment. This project, unequal by its sheer size, was made possible in the new plant when the Group could redesign a number of improved processes. It is part of the environmental policies implemented by Renault in 1995".

"A new industrial approach with a commitment to sustainability requires results that are above classical solutions or processes. With its plant in Tangiers, Veolia Environment demonstrates its capacity to propose new avant-garde methods that break with traditional solutions to fulfill the expectations of its clients", states Stéphane Caine, Director of Industrial Markets and New Activity Sectors with Veolia Environment. "To attain this level of performance, Renault and Veolia Environment realized beforehand a true co-design team approach".

TANGIERS PLANT: IMPORTANT BENEFICIAL CONSEQUENCES FOR MOROCCO

Commercially located in Morocco since 1928, Renault is the leader of the automobile market in the country with its brands Renault and Dacia. Having already a production unit in Casablanca (SOMACA), the Group in 2008 began the construction of a vast industrial complex comprised of an assembly plant with access to the platform harbour facility at Tanger Med Port. It was designed to complete the entire manufacturing cycle needed for a Renault industrial park facility built for economy model vehicles because of the low-cost Logan platform.

Given an investment of 1.1 billion Euros, this new Moroccan national gem is located on a site of 314 ha in the special economic zone of Tangiers-Mediterranean in the north of the Kingdom. Its production capacity is huge: one vehicle every two minutes.

Morocco Now Deeply Rooted in the Automobile Industry

At the inaugural ceremony for the Tangiers plant, Carlos Ghosn uttered, *"Enthusiasm can move mountains"*. In fact, for Renault to build the largest plant on the south shore of the Mediterranean, in Africa and in the Arab world, moving mountains was almost needed, with indefatigable enthusiasm coupled with a very strong desire to succeed. The mountain was indeed lofty, but the enthusiasm even more important. In effect, the site is immense considering it took two years of heavy work to modify the 300 hectares that were located in a zone considered difficult terrain. The rivers also had to be diverted and channelled to prevent the violent rains in that region from ravaging the soil. This was possible because of unwavering support by the Moroccan government. *"Renault and Nissan share grand visions for industrial development with the Moroccan Kingdom. Thanks to the keen interest by Renault and its partners, our plant is on track to becoming a new reference worldwide for the automobile industry"*, affirmed Mr. Ghosn.

For his part, Abdelkader Aamara, Minister of Industry, Commerce and New Technologies for the Moroccan government, mentioned that in addition to the important role played in reenergising the northern region, such an industrial facility will act as a beacon for the country in attracting other investments. *"Because of this project, Morocco is now on the map of the automobile industry"*, said the Minister.

Besides the transfer of technologies, the Minister added, this project allowed us to draw new renowned international parts manufacturers, whose investments are estimated to be 1.27 billion Euros. *"Renault-Tangiers Med will continue to improve the commercial trade balance of Morocco, through the annual increase in the value of exports in the automobile sector of more than 38.5 billion dirhams*[41]*"*, explained Abdelkader Aâmara.

Considering the grant of free land, the exoneration of company taxation, and a training center entirely financed by the Moroccan state, for some these concessions may seem exaggerated. "To have, one must learn to give. Morocco did well in negotiating this project and the future will prove it" reassures the minister. When it comes to assurances, Carlos Ghosn also had an earful when addressing his fellow businessmen who criticized the location of the Renault plants. *"Considerable French engineering and companies are involved in this project. For each vehicle built in Tangiers, 800 Euros are returned to France, approximately 630 million Euros per year"*, states Mr. Ghosn.

An Essential Employment Center for People in the Region

As for *"job creation"*, always a cornerstone with projects of this size and of great importance for the population in the northern region of the kingdom, the plant will generate no less than 6,000 direct jobs and some 30,000 indirect jobs. In short, it is a substantial benefit for the local population.

---

[41]1 EUR = 11.132 MAD at 17/04/12

"The rate of hiring is consistent with a coherent rhythm and is synchronized with production requirements. We are currently at 2,000 employees with 230 technicians and engineers from Europe (France, Spain, Romania and Turkey) who will provide an experienced workforce to assist in the proper start-up of the plant", a fact that was recently mentioned in the plant newsletter, written by Michel Faivre-Duboz, Director General of Renault in Morocco. The new plant, the most competitive facility in the French group, figures prominently in the company's plans to make it a platform for the production and export of automobiles. In fact, 85% of its production is destined for export, notably to Eastern and Western Europe, Asia, and Africa.

Taking into Account the Needs of the Region

On a wider front, the company initiated a proactive and dynamic dialogue along with joint actions with local players, communities, associations, non-profit organizations, and partners. Access to education and training, equal opportunity and the promotion of diversity, and the security of all concerned who follow the path – these are the strategic axes of the policies for Social Responsibility of the Renault Group – and which Renault has decided put into play locally in Morocco.

> *"Once it was decided that the Tangiers plant would be built in the Melloussa community, we watched over it as the plant established roots with the region. With help from Planet Finance, and in consultation with institutional players and local associations, we conducted a diagnostic of the needs of the region. We uncovered a strong desire by the local population to have access to mobility, especially in schools and education. This is why we signed a partnership agreement with the "Maison de la jeune fille de Melloussa" and to which we made a grant for a postgraduate degree dedicated to school transport. We also provided the school with a sports field and a library."*

"In Casablanca, the city where we built our historic industrial sites of Somaca and Renault in Morocco, we chose to promote access to education through the meritocracy by signing an agreement with the "Fondation Marocaine de l'Étudiant" that allows those with a bachelor's degree, issued by social centers, to have access to higher education by means of a system of bursaries and Mentoring".

"Whether in Tangiers or in Casablanca, our local CSR policy will be reinforced by other actions in the months to come", as explained by Mr. Michel Faivre-Duboz, Director General of the Group Renault in Morocco[42].

---

[42] CSR Newsletter of the Renault Group, April-2012 available on: www.renault.com

ANALYSIS AND INTERPRETATION OF RESULTS

The above case study is very interesting in that it shows the enormous possibilities that new technologies offer companies, making them more effective and efficient in attaining their objectives while remaining at the cutting edge of environmental protection. It also demonstrates a perfect example of a successful collaboration between a multinational company and the local authorities of the host developing country. Based on the theoretical model we elaborated, we shall proceed to analyse the information collected by following the identical flow in which they were collected throughout the organization and the plant. We shall therefore list the four dimensions of CSR according to Caroll along with the interpretations that we are able to extract in order to explain them.

ECONOMIC RESPONSIBILITY: A CAREFULLY STUDIED INVESTMENT

The choice of Tangiers was not by chance. The decision taken by Renault to build in the special economic zone of Tanger-Med in the north of Morocco offered numerous opportunities for the company to remain in sync with its strategic objectives. For observers, this megaproject validated the Moroccan *offshore* model that included a complete package of taxation, land, accessibility, and a transfer of knowledge that allowed the Royal Kingdom to become competitive with countries such as Romania and Brazil[43].

ADVANTAGES OBTAINED BY MOROCCO

As summarized by the Moroccan Agency for Development and Investments[44], the reasons for investing in Morocco, which Renault surely benefits from, are:

---

[43]   www.lesafriques.com/actualite/l-usine-renault-tanger-nouveau-moteur-de-l-offshoring-maro.
      html?Itemid =89 viewed on 19/04/2012
[44] For more details, please consult: www.invest.gov.ma

COST COMPETITIVENESS

At only 14 km from Europe, Morocco has positioned itself as a competitive export platform, notably:

- Lower salaries: The average salary in Morocco is $327 per month, almost 10 times less than the average salary in Spain;
- Competitive export costs: 577 $/container according to data by the World Bank , the 6th most competitive in the world;
- Lower fiscal costs: The total taxes paid by companies represents 42% of their profits, the most competitive rate in the region;

Strong and Stable Economic Fundamentals

Preserving a macroeconomic equilibrium is a major preoccupation of public policy decision makers. A number of actions and structural reforms were undertaken in order to ensure the country was on the right path for strong and durable economic growth:

- Access to a new level of growth: A continuous economic growth at an average rate of 5% between 2005-2010;
- Resilient to crises: In the context of a world economic and financial crisis, the Moroccan economy showed its strength of 4.9% GDP growth in 2009, the strongest rate of growth in the entire Mediterranean region;
- Controlling inflation: The Moroccan inflation stands at about 2% despite the increase in the price of oil and primary materials;
- Reducing the level of debt: The total Treasury debt was reduced by 24 pts. between 2000 and 2010 to a level of 49% of the 2010 GDP;
- A growth based on interior demand and public investments: Household spending increased by 8% per year between 2004 and 2010 to reach 442 billion DH (52 billion USD), while public investment almost tripled during the same period to 167 billion DH (20 billion USD).

Access to a Market of More Than a Billion Consumers

Thanks to a number of international agreements, Morocco offers investors free trade access to a market of 55 countries representing a billion consumers and 60% of the world GDP.

- Morocco/European Union: Morocco is the first country on the southern coast of the Mediterranean to benefit from advanced status in its relationships with the European Union;
- Morocco/United-States: The free trade agreement with the United-States (sixth largest economic partner of Morocco);
- Mediterranean: Signed in February 2004, the Agadir Agreement between Morocco, Egypt, Jordan, and Tunisia allowed for lowering non-tariff based barriers and the establishment of a gradual free trade zone;
- In addition to these accords, Morocco signed agreements with Turkey and the rest of the Arab world. Soon, Canada will be included in its list of partners with a free trade agreement, one which is in advanced exploratory discussions;

Infrastructures on a Par with International Standards

For more than a decade, Morocco has been undertaking large infrastructure projects designed to meet international standards. For the new Renault plant, it will have the advantage of new installations at the port of Tangiers-Mediterranean[45] that was officially opened in 2007 with a global capacity of 3 million containers (8 million in 2016) and professional grade land of more than 2,000 hectares that completed a harbour network already composed of 11 ports that meet international standards.

Skilled and Efficient Human Resources

In Morocco, human resources represent a major competitive asset to investors and the creation of value-added services: training, cultural acceptance, knowledge of different languages and technologies, esprit-de-corps in their work, and the ability to adapt to changes in competitive activities and salary costs:

- A young, active population: Out of a total population of 32 million inhabitants, 64 % are less than 34 years of age, providing 12 million active persons.
- Qualified human resources: 16 Universities and 170 private higher-study centers – 370,000 students in combined higher-study public/private – 40,000 diplomas issued by higher-study universities, with10,000 engineers.

---

[45] For more details on the Tangiers-Med port, please consult: www.tmsa.ma

- Large linguistic abilities: Almost 20 million inhabitants speak French – More than 5 million speak Spanish – with strong English speaking abilities among the youth and management employees;
- Professional training adapted to needs: 300 professional training centers – 200,000 trainees/yr. in the 2009-2012 period – Training grants that can pay as much as 65,000 DH per person recruited;

Ambitious Sector-Based Strategies

A series of sector-based plans, designed to ensure a strong and sustainable economic growth that will create wealth, were implemented by public authorities. This dynamic development distinguishes itself by its novel approach in contracting-out and a public-private sector partnership advocating an increased and concerted participation by the private sector in developing the strategies and the sector-based policies and financing the projects, allowing the State to refocus its role on the prerogatives of regulation.

These plans are part of a double logic of modernizing traditional sectors such as agriculture, fisheries, and mines but in a manner geared towards the development of innovative sectors such as renewable energies, logistics, automobile manufacturing, aeronautics, and strong value-added services where Morocco offers genuine competitive advantages.

A FAVOURABLE BUSINESS ENVIRONMENT

In order to encourage investment, a particular interest is centered on improving business climate. A number of mechanisms aimed at reinforcing competition and transparency were implemented and include:

- Simplification of administrative procedures involving companies;
- Reinforcing the system of business laws (competition, free price roaming, economic interest groups, industrial and intellectual property rights etc.);
- Improving regulatory transparency;
- Developing and modernizing financial markets;
- Creation of a National Committee on Business Environment
- Creation of the Central Bureau for the Prevention of Corruption;
- Creation of the Moroccan Office of Intellectual and Commercial Property;
- Promotion of the Charter of Social Responsibility for Companies;

ADVANTAGES OF THE TANGIERS PLANT

So as not to limit ourselves to generalities, we shall now analyse the performance realized by the Renault Group, specifically its new production platform in a geo-strategically located site, and whose impact on nature is almost negligible:

Low Cost Resources

Renault gained important advantages even before beginning production. In fact, it was able to benefit from the grant of land, offered graciously by the Moroccan government, of 314 ha and the company will also benefit from a total exoneration of corporate taxes as well as border duty for a period of five years.

In addition, in Tangiers, Renault and Morocco jointly created an Institute for Learning Trades in the Automobile Industry (IFMIA), which is financed exclusively by the Moroccan State, for plant staff as well as for equipment suppliers thus providing an enormous contribution in terms of training a workforce that will be available for the plant start-up. In France, the Global Training Center (GTC) in Flins accepted 168 people working for this project to train the trainers, management staff, and plant technicians.

Once production begins, the plant will have a substantial advantage because of its proximity to Tangiers-Med, the largest African port and one of the most modern logistical platforms in the Mediterranean. The port is situated at 14 km from Spain, on the Strait of Gibraltar, in a strategic location on the passageway between Asia, Europe, North America, and South America.

As previously mentioned, Morocco has the 6th most competitive rate in the world for export taxes. An important detail when knowing that the production output from the plant in Tangiers shall be destined for export, notably to Europe, Asia, and Africa.

Increased Efficiency

Moreover, the desire to showcase this plant on the world scene as a first with its objective of "zero carbon" and "zero liquid industrial waste", Renault is not only protecting the planet, but realizing significant economies in all matters of energy. For example, the thermal energy needs for the plant in Tangiers will be decreased by 35% (more than 40 GWh of PCI annually) compared to an equivalent plant of equal production capacity.

Another advantage of this "eco" plant is that it will be the source of three new models; namely, the mono-space Lodgy, a utilitarian, and a third model still kept secret. We have already discussed the importance for a company to be recognized as socially responsible by the local parties. This recognition translates into a favourable reaction towards the company in not only the field of energy consumption, but also in the field of human resources (hiring), and also investments (Sen et al., 2006). In addition, since we are talking about three new models, it has been said that an equally favourable reaction will be bestowed on new products proposed in the marketplace and received with a positive attitude by customers (Duong and Robert-Demontrond, 2004; Brown and Dacin, 1997).

A Satisfactory Performance

As we have previously shown, measuring performance means measuring the three dimensions that comprise it; namely, economy, efficiency, and effectiveness (Bouquin, 2004). We must remember that the economy consists of obtaining resources at the lowest cost, that efficiency is a result of maximizing the quantity of products or services obtained from a particular unit of resource, that profitability are two kinds of efficiency, and finally that effectiveness is the result of realizing the objectives and the final outcome, so desired at the onset (Dohou-Renaud and Berland, 2007).

Now, we have seen how Renault obtained its resources at the lowest cost via the contributions of the Moroccan State that granted the land at no cost, provided tax-free exemptions, and assumed 100% of the cost for training human resources. As well, we have estimated how the anticipated profitability and productivity will be increased due to the site of the production facility and the positive impact of its world-renowned brand. Finally, regarding the evaluation of the effectiveness, it is impossible at this moment in time to assess considering the plant has only recently been inaugurated.

Moreover, as other displays of economic responsibility by Renault vis-à-vis its partners that should not be neglected, we should mention the 6,000 direct employment and some 30,000 indirect jobs, which all generate wealth that will be created by this ambitious project. Each job is a synonym of wealth creation and an improvement in the lives of the local population.

Based on these observations, we can conclude that Renault has respected its economic responsibilities vis-à-vis its partners.

> **Conclusion 1: The decision by a company to invest in developing countries positively affects its economic responsibility with an acceptable profitability.**

LEGAL RESPONSIBILITIES: THE MOROCCAN INSTITUTIONAL METHOD

Briefly, as mentioned earlier, this category includes expectations of complying with the legal system. Moreover, society expects companies to fulfill their economic mission as per the framework of requirements established by the legislative system and signed into law (Branco and Rodrigues, 2007).

Labaronne and Gana-Oueslati, in their comparative analysis of the institutional framework of CSR in Morocco and Tunisia (Labaronne and Gana-Oueslati, 2011), lists an exhaustive panorama of Moroccan institutional methodology. According to them, it was at the summit for the "Complete Guide to Investment" (Intégrales de l'investissement) organized by the Directorate of Foreign Investments in October 2005 that Moroccan authorities clearly expressed their desire to adhere to the values of CSR. Later, this agreement was written in a concrete manner as part of the judicial framework, a means to normalize and label the agreement.

THE JUDICIAL FRAMEWORK

The judicial framework was progressively modified to take into account this new set of CSR values (M'Hamdi and Trid, 2009).

The Rights of Workers responds to the attachment of fundamental human rights. Its implementation has allowed for conformity with international conventions ratified by Morocco. This evolution answers the wishes expressed by the economic partners in the country, financial backers, and the ILO.

Human Rights are recognized on the institutional level with the creation of the Consultative Committee on Human Rights, plus the Authority on Equality and Reconciliation. They are the guarantors for the respect of the universal values of man. They conform to the legal framework of international agreements. They adjudicate questions regarding equality and non-discrimination, the protection of children, freedom of association, and the condition of women that oversees a variety of subjects such as civil matters, personal status, the right to work, and penal rights.

Environmental Rights aims to ensure the coherence of the environmental framework both at the national and international levels. Specifically, they must:

- Ensure the implementation of a legislative and regulatory framework to protect and improve the environment, while reconciling the imperative to preserve the environment and the need for sustainable socio-economic development;
- To oversee judicial coherence over all environmental texts, both existing and those to be adopted, as well as overseeing their implementation;

The law regarding environmental protection and value-added improvements (law 11-03, June 19, 2003) encourages authorities to respect international agreements on the environment when preparing plans and development programs as well as environmental legislation. It adopts the principles of "users pay" and "polluters pay". It wants companies to voluntarily identify administrative deficiencies when their work and/or construction site lacks appropriate infrastructures, and when the institutional means of surveillance, alerts, training, etc., are insufficient.

The following laws are also part of the legislation:

- 13-03 Air pollution
- 12-03 Environmental impact studies
- 10-95 Water
- 08-01 Exploitation of quarry sites
- 28-00 Waste management disposal

MOROCCAN STANDARDIZATION

The judicial framework[46] for the standardization system was implemented in 1970, with the creation of SNIMA (Service de Normalisation Industrielle Marocaine / Moroccan Industrial Standardization Service), that reports to the

---

[46] Dahir n° 1.70.157 of July 30, 1970 relative to the industrial standardization regarding the research on quality and improvements in productivity, modified in 1993. Decree n° 2.70.314 of October 8, 1970 fixed the composition and attributes of the organizations for industrial standardization. Decree n° 2.93.530 of September 20, 1993 adopted relative to the quality and the certificate of conformity with Moroccan norms.

Ministry of Industry and Commerce. The three institutes for Moroccan standardization are the Inter-Ministry Senior Advisory for Quality and Productivity, the Technical Committee for Standardization, and the Moroccan Industrial Standardization Services.

(Le Conseil Supérieur Interministériel de la Qualité et de la Productivité (CSIQP) ; Le Comité Techniques de Normalisation (CTNs) ; Les Services de Normalisation Industrielle Marocaine (SNIMA))

Besides European and international standards, Morocco has already published more than 3,700 norms covering different aspects in different sectors. It has obtained technical references for the certification of national systems and quality control. National standards relative to the principal management systems also were established for issues regarding CSR.

Besides, Morocco is governed by 80 technical committees that oversee different sectors[47] of the economy that include manufacturers, end users, laboratories, universities, administrations, and consumer associations.

THE LABEL GCMC FOR MOROCCAN CSR

Moroccan companies that benefit from the label of the General Confederation of Moroccan Companies (CGEM / GCMC) are recognized for their support of CSR. They are known for observing, defending, and promoting the universal principles of social responsibility and Sustainable Development in their economic activities, social relationships, and more generally for their contribution to wealth creation.

This confederation charter is written in conformity with the fundamental principles of the Kingdom's Constitution and the requirements of international treaties, regarding respect for fundamental human rights, environmental protection, sound governance, and loyal competitiveness.

The label CGEM is granted for a period of three years to companies based in Morocco, as members of the confederation, without discrimination to size, sector, products, or services.

Companies that are granted this label obtain advantages and special treatment from administrative partners (customs, internal revenue, social insurance) or banking (The Moroccan Farm Credit, The group "Banques Populaires", the Moroccan Bank for Commerce and Industry) in the form of

---

[47]Labaronne and Gana-Oueslati counted 11 technical committees in the fields of chemistry and para-chemistry, 2 in textile and leather, 18 in food-processing, 14 in the field of mechanics, 6 in electric, 6 in BTP and 11 in quality and security.

preferential tariffs, simplified procedures, relaxation of controls, personal management, and faster treatment of dossiers.

At such a level, in order to evaluate the legal responsibility of a company, we stipulated earlier that the required conformity supposes the existence of standards and regulations to which companies are held accountable, and that in a CDW such as Morocco we would evaluate the existence or lack thereof of such a mechanism susceptible of managing the activities and potential machinations of every economic entity, whether national or foreign, working on local soil.

We can now state with certainty that the Moroccan institutional framework not only exists but also, because of its judicial arsenal, and its mechanisms for standards and labels, appears to us to be substantive and, in addition, is centered on social responsibility (Labaronne and Gana-Oueslati, 2011).

By taking the decision to invest in Tangiers, Renault was not moving into unknown territory. The Group has been present in Morocco since 1928 and we can be certain as to its behaviour in respecting the laws of the land otherwise its non-respect would have terminated all activities, pure and simple. Moreover, Renault is already the owner of a production plant in Casablanca (SOMACA) and is considered the leader of the automobile market with its brands Renault and Dacia.

> **Conclusion 2: the choice of a company to invest in a CDW requires it to effectively respect the existing local rules and conform to them.**

ETHICAL RESPONSIBILITIES: ZERO CO$_2$, ZERO INDUSTRIAL LIQUID WASTE

Taking the directives of standard ISO26000 as inspiration, and considering the nature of our case study, we have demonstrated respect for the environment as a manifestation of commitment or ethical responsibility on behalf of Renault. The ISO26000 allows for three types of action to answer this question: preventing pollution, utilizing sustainable resources, and attenuating climatic changes.

We have dedicated a large part of our description of Renault as an ecologically responsible company that has realized a considerable feat with its new production plant in Tangiers as proof. We also described in considerable detail, with data in hand, how this new industrial facility in Morocco met the three types of actions as per ISO26000.

A brief recap shows that with the Renault-Nissan plant in Tangiers, the Kingdom of Morocco has embraced the most *"green"* automobile plant in the world with respect to environmental impacts. The impacts have been reduced to levels never seen: 98% reduction in CO_2 emissions when compared to an identical production/assembly plant elsewhere in the world. Concretely, more than 135,000 tons of CO_2 emissions will be avoided every year, and water requirements will be reduced by 70%, which will help conserve the natural resources in Morocco. In the section "Legal Responsibilities", we have shown that the Moroccan institutional framework is well prepared and favourable to matters of social responsibility (Labaronne and Gana-Oueslati, 2011). It would have sufficed for Renault to simply respect Moroccan national laws and regulations to satisfy the legal requirements and be seen as responsible. However, Renault, in its quest to seek new revolutionary processes, not only limited its external negatives, but also almost totally suppressed them. It even contributed to reforesting the region with plantations of eucalyptus wood that will be cultivated in 4 years in a short rotation. Besides, the plant in Tangiers shows a perfect convergence of Renault's vision with that promoted by the Kingdom of Morocco that demonstrates an almost particular zeal for promoting renewable energies notably solar and Aeolian. The interest it shows towards the development of such energies comes from its desire to reduce its dependence on fossil fuels and to contribute to the international effort to fight climate change. Besides the realization of many Aeolian parks, and the start of construction of a solar-powered station at Ouarzazate in southern Morocco, the major contribution by Morocco will be the Desertec mega-project that will generate electricity from solar energy and will be the first central solar-powered generating station implemented in the Kingdom by 2012, for an investment of 800 million dollars.

> **Conclusion 3: the decision by a company to invest in a CDW obliges it to act in an ethical manner notably by respecting the environment.**

DISCRETIONARY RESPONSIBILITIES: REGIONAL ANCHOR

Renault and its subsidiaries host numerous philanthropic activities throughout the world education and training, diversity, road security, and sustainable mobility to name a few. The total amount spent on these activities cost 10.4 million euros.

In Morocco, as explained by Michel Faivre-Duboz, Director General of Renault in Morocco, as soon as the plant was inaugurated in Tangiers in the community of Melloussa, Renault began anchoring the plant with the region by associating with institutional players to realize a diagnostic on the needs of the local population.

Consequently, the actions taken on the social and societal fronts are numerous and with targeted consensual efforts, better effectiveness can be obtained:

- Automobile Training Institute for salaried plant workers;
- Creation of the local network *Women @ Renault*;
- Grants and mentoring of young stock-exchange brokers from the Moroccan
- Foundation for Students;
- Equipment for transportation purposes for young girls in boarding school in Melloussa (region of Tangiers where the plant is located);
- Initiating the educational program "Security and mobility for all";

As a reminder, in order to evaluate this last category on social responsibilities, we refer to responsibilities that are purely voluntary or philanthropic where they represent roles assumed by companies on their own initiative, for which there are no specific expectations by society as there exists with ethical responsibilities (Branco and Rodrigues, 2007). The objective is to decide what specific activities or philanthropic contributions can best offer the most useful return to society (Jamali and Mirshak, 2007; Jamali, 2007).

In fact, to clarify the very expectations by society, Renault proceeded to conduct an evaluation of the needs of the local population by including different institutional and associate players in the region. This collaboration was fruitful in producing better effectiveness, a result of good consensual targeting efforts.

Conclusion 4: the philanthropic actions undertaken by a company in a CDW positively affects their social responsibility.

The four conclusions mentioned in the above study provide us with a positive and optimistic impression regarding the societal performance of the

Renault Group in the context of Morocco. In order to present a flow diagram of the analytical results, we have opted for a CSR pyramid of this company adapted from that proposed by Carroll (1991). As with a real pyramid, the base represents economic responsibilities and must be solid and consistent to support the upper levels that will be layered until the apex is reached, shown here by discretionary responsibilities. As previously explained, this conceptualization implies that the four types of responsibility are additive (Jamali and Mirshak, 2007; Jamali, 2007), and it is by grouping them that we can analyse the global societal performance of the entire organization.

CONCLUSION

The case study lets us assume that it is very possible to have organizations that are socially responsible in developing countries. It confirms in a way the nomadic and malleable character of the CSR concept (Acquier and Gond, 2007) since we can see it in action in a country other than those who are known to be already favourable at the onset.

The first conclusion that stems from our research states that the decision of a company to invest in a developing country positively affects its economic responsibility while providing for an acceptable return on investment or profitability. This result reinforces previous studies conducted to analyse the existing relationships between CSR practices and the financial performance of companies that have demonstrated a positive correlation between the two (Sen et al., 2006; Tsoutsoura, 2004; Hillman and Keim, 2001; Waddock and Graves, 1997; Brown and Dacin, 1997).

The second conclusion shows us that the decision of a company to invest in a developing country effectively requires it to respect and abide existing local regulations. Throughout this case study, we have seen how an EMN, present in the CDW host country since 1927, honours its legal responsibilities *required* by society (Windsor, 2001) by obliging it to fulfill its economic mission according to the framework of rules established by the legislative system and signed into law (Branco and Rodrigues, 2007).

In fact, this conclusion contradicts the remarks made by certain authors who believe that, in the context of a developing country identified as having a weak institutional framework, expectations in matters of social responsibility should be more modest *(Dobers and Halme, 2009;* Jamali and Mirshak, 2007). Therefore, it would be more prudent to no longer include developing countries in the "same basket" considering we were in a country clearly marked as being in the developing third world, but one that had equipped itself with an elaborate and functional judicial system with its own mechanisms of standards and labels in harmony with international norms. Some researchers have gone as far as saying that it is based on social responsibility (Labaronne and Gana-Oueslati, 2011).

The third conclusion confirms that the decision of a company to invest in a developing country forces it effectively to act in an ethical manner notably by respecting the environment. Without restating details previously provided, the new Renault production unit inaugurated in Morocco depicts, for example, a much more "favourable image" of outsourcing than that which is typically provided by companies exploiting oil and gas (Campbell, 2008; Boele et al. 2001).

At the same time, we note that Renault places considerable emphasis on environmental matters. This agrees with the conclusions of Sweeney and Coughlan (2008) who stipulate that, in the automobile industry, the accent of CSR depended squarely on environmental protection. On the other hand, these statements are quite different than the arguments advanced by Mitnick (2000) who supported the view that companies having a negative impact on a particular domain of CSR (environment) will not advertise it on a large scale but rather will highlight other fields where they have a positive impact, such as philanthropic grants.

This case study has shown us the image of an automobile company that *assumes* its responsibility (environmental footprint in their vehicles and infrastructure requirements) as an international automobile manufacturer by improving its products and by conducting research on a more effective production system overall.

Finally, the fourth and last conclusion resulting from our research shows that philanthropic actions made by a company in a developing country positively affects its social responsibility. Contrary to other *predatory* multinationals, we see that Renault is attempting to fully integrate itself in the milieu where it is installed and, far from exploiting the region, it is immersing itself in its new environment, exactly as predicted by Martinet and Payaud (2011).

Furthermore, beyond the above conclusions, there are certain points that draw our interest and which we would like to discuss to hopefully enrich this work and bring our opinions and ideas to the debate on CSR and developing countries.

Although we demonstrated that this particular case study clearly showed the nomadic character and the malleable concept of CSR (Acquier and Gond,

2007), it would be pretentious to believe that the CSR concept in itself was the object of local *re-appropriation* or *re-interpretation* (Acquier and Gond, 2007; Gond, 2006; Gond and Boxenbaum, 2004) because we do not see specific adaptations to the Moroccan context but a respect for universally known standards, formalized by the norm ISO26000. Nonetheless, it was discussed at a certain level to take into consideration the specific expectations of the local population and use them as a basis for their reflections in determining their CSR actions. This can be viewed, in itself, as a form of "CSR Innovation" (Halme and Laurila, 2009) that organizations are invited to study in the context of developing countries.

We therefore saw how Renault undertook social problems (isolation of the population, emancipation of women, deficiencies in the school system, etc.) as a source of new initiatives along with adequate measures to resolve them (transportation grants, a social network for women, a sport field, library, grants, etc.). This was possible because of local involvement in the choice of actions to take and because of the willingness of Renault to create a regional anchor around its new plant.

However, what remains most interesting is to see how a large multinational corporation, instead of being content with establishing an "ordinary" production unit in a developing country, decides to invest its technical and technological expertise to design and build a "world first" referring to its ecological footprint. That an MNC would make such an effort to make a difference is without doubt an encouraging sign and sets the bar much higher for future investors who should view this as an example of enterprise-societal cooperation.

A priori, Renault is in line for achieving this highly ambitious compromise between the imperatives of economic viability and the expectations of different partners by respecting as much as possible their specificity (Martinet and Payaud, 2011). Consequently, we would be even closer to this harmonious equilibrium between the economics, the social, and the environmental (Martinet and Payaud, 2011; Biwolé et al., 2008; Spence et al., 2007; Ernult and Ashta, 2007).

Starting with this theory, we could say that Renault tends to enter the field of sustainability by seeking equilibrium between the three dimensions of SD. This research is clearly manifested by its *holistic and integrated* approach to building its plant. It is an approach that is seen in its voluntary and formalized integration of the three SD dimensions in its strategy (Biwolé et al., 2008; Spence et al., 2007).

In the same line of thinking, the results we obtained in this study contradict the belief according to which CSR and the developing countries limit themselves to philanthropic activities and programs (Jamali and Mirshak, 2007; Jamali, 2007). Quite the contrary, the strategic aspects of CSR were never ignored by Renault when studying its investment, thus favouring a convergence between its interests and those of society, and a reconciliation of the social and economic objectives (Porter and Kramer, 2006).

Because of this approach, known as *"holistic and integrated"*, Renault is on the proper path to experiment and determine the most desirable scenario possible for all commercial organizations for profit, which consist of delivering shareholder value while favouring societal value (Branco and Rodrigues, 2007; Jamali, 2007; Porter and Kramer, 2003; Drucker, 1984). However, we will be careful to leave these affirmations in the conditional sense since we must wait some time before judging the respect for promises made versus promises delivered.

In conclusion, we have attempted throughout this paper to answer our problematic supporting the possibility of an emergence of the CSR concept in developing countries. We began by listing a complete overview, as faithfully as possible, of the state of current knowledge on the subject, in a broad sense, and then we concentrated our research on CSR in the developing countries.

It turns out that the concept is far from being new, or in a temporary mode, but a theoretical development that finds its roots in religious beliefs including even teachings from antiquity. CSR since then is presented as an *open, multiform concept in construction* and still presents challenges to researchers. The first is finding a *unique* definition acceptable by all. In the context of CSR, the state of knowledge on the subject continues to progress; however, the lack of assimilation by local organizations is still deplorable as is the refusal to observe its principles by certain foreign firms.

Nevertheless, our particular case study, exemplified by the inauguration of a *green* production plant in Morocco, leaves us on an optimistic note and weakens the fatalism presented by MNC operating in less developed countries as *predators*.

It is true that our study is based on a single company and in a single country; however, we readily recognize that it is a limitation on our research, but we decided to present this case study for its originality and for its contrast with preconceived ideas on outsourcing practices. To portray it as idyllic or to apply generalized conclusions to all MNC and/or developing countries projects would be deliberately deceiving, and pretentious.

There is a quote that says: "All generalizations are false, including this one!" In other words, we must always nuance the information obtained and not allow ourselves to be *conditioned* by those who are prejudiced. By standing back before conducting any analysis, and maintaining objectivity at all times, we will then come closer to the truth.

The same objectivity made us realize, at the end of our discussion on the results, the need to remind the reader that the conclusions reached are conditional. Since, in our opinion, it is too soon to evaluate, with certainty, the promises proposed and kept by Renault, even though they are laudable and very attractive.

Nevertheless, let us keep in mind that this project was promoted as a *world first* and was first during the fifth edition of the "*Sustainable Energy European awards* 2011" organized by the European Union in the category "Production". This distinction provides it with a certain credibility regarding the feasibility of its objectives, and encourages us to believe that this project has strong chances of becoming a reality rather than a simple utopian promise.

Whatever the case, it would be useful to further contribute to this work by an eventual empirical study that would enrich our knowledge on the subject. Our work then would be considered as a first step in this quest to widen our knowledge base. We view our participation as that of a sentry that enlightens the road for those who wish to continue on the same path. Finally, we hope that the reader of this research study has seen a coherent path and has found conclusive answers to his questions.

REFERENCES

Acquier et Gond (2007), Aux sources de la responsabilité sociale de l'entreprise : à la (re)découverte d'un ouvrage fondateur, Social Responsibilities of the Businessman d'Howard Bowen, Finance contrôle Stratégie, Vol. 10, n° 2, juin 2007

Biwolé, Spence et Ben Boubaker Gherib (2008), Stratégies de développement durable dans les PME : Une étude exploratoire auprès des PME camerounaises, Communication présentée au 9ème CIFEPME, Louvain-la-Neuve (Belgique)

Boele, Fabig et Wheeler (2001), Shell, Nigeria and the Ogoni. A study in unsustainable development: II. Corporate social responsibility and 'stakeholder management' versus a rights-based approach to sustainable development, Sustainable Development, Vol.9 (3)

Bouquin (2004), Le contrôle de gestion, Presses Universitaires de France, Collection Gestion, 6ème édition, Paris, 508 p.

Branco et Rodrigues (2007), Positioning Stakeholder Theory within the Debate on Corporate Social Responsibility, Electronic Journal of Business Ethics and Organization Studies, Vol. 12, No. 1

Brown et Dacin (1997), The Company and the Product: Corporate Associations and Consumer Product Responses, Journal of Marketing, Vol. 61, No. 1

Campbell (2008), l'exploitation minière en Afrique : enjeux de responsabilité et d'imputabilité, Présentation faite dans le cadre de la conférence : exploitation minière et développement durable en Afrique (www.ieim.uqam.ca)

Carroll (1991), The Pyramid of Corporate Social Responsibility: Toward the Moral Management of Organizational Stakeholders, Business Horizons, Vol. 34, No. 4,

Dobers et Halme (2009), Corporate Social Responsibility and Developing Countries, Corporate Social Responsibility and Environmental Management, Vol. 16

Dohou-Renaud et Berland (2007), Mesure de la performance globale des entreprises, Actes du Congrès Annuel de l'Association Francophone de Comptabilité, Poitiers, France, Mai 2007

Drucker (1984), The new meaning of corporate social responsibility, California Management Review 262

Ernult et Ashta (2007), Développement durable, responsabilité sociétale de l'entreprise, théorie des parties prenantes : Évolution et perspectives, Cahiers du CEREN 21

Gond et Boxenbaum (2004), Studying the Diffusion of Socially Responsible Investment : Bricolage and Translation across Cultural Contexts, Working Paper du LIRHE, n° 398

Halme et Laurila (2009), Philantropy, Integration or Innovation? Exploring the Financial and Societal Outcomes of Different Types of Corporate Responsibility. Journal of Business Ethics, 84

Hillman et Keim (2001), Shareholder value, stakeholder management, and social issues: What's the bottom line? Strategic Management Journal, Vol.22

Jamali (2007). The Case for Strategic Corporate Social Responsibility in Developing Countries. Business and Society Review. 112

Jamali et Mirshak (2007), Corporate Social Responsibility (CSR): Theory and Practice in a Developing Country Context, Journal of Business Ethics, 72, Springer 2006

Labaronne et Gana-Oueslati (2011), Analyse comparative Maroc-Tunisie du cadre institutionnel de la RSE dans les PME. Management & Avenir, n° 43

M'hamdi et Trid (2009), La responsabilité sociale de l'entreprise au Maroc: une étude empirique auprès des petites et moyennes entreprises de la région de Fes Boulemane, Colloque sur La vulnérabilité des TPE et des PME dans un environnement mondialisé, INRPME 2009

Martinet et Payaud (2011), Capacité des pauvres et stratégies RSE-BOP, EURISTIK

Mitnick, B. (2000). Commitment, revelation, and the testaments of belief: The metrics ofmeasurement of corporate social performance. Business & Society 39, no. 4

Porter et Kramer (2006) The link between competitive advantage and corporate social responsibility. Harvard Business Review, December 2006

Sen, Bhattacharya et Korschun (2006), The Role of Corporate Social Responsibility in Strengthening Multiple Stakeholder Relationships: A Field Experiment, Journal of the Academy of Marketing Science, Volume 34, No. 2,

Spence, Ben Boubaker Gherib et Ondoua (2007), Une étude exploratoire des fondements du degré d'engagement des PME dans le développement durable, Journées scientifiques de l'entrepreneuriat de l'AUF, Antananarivo, Madagascar.

Sweeney et Coughlan (2008). Do different industries report corporate social responsibility differently? An investigation through the lens of stakeholder theory. Journal of Marketing Communications, Vol.14

Tsoutsoura (2004), Corporate Social Responsibility and Financial Performance, Applied Financial Project, Haas School of Business, University of California at Berkeley

Waddock et Graves (1997), The corporate social performance – financial performance link, Strategic Management Journal, Vol.18

Windsor (2001), The future of corporate social responsibility, The International Journal of Organizational Analysis, 9(3)

In: Multinational's CSR Practices ...   ISBN: 978-1-63463-479-3
Editor: Alidou Ouedraogo   © 2015 Nova Science Publishers, Inc.

Chapter 3

MNCS AND ANTI-CORRUPTION PRACTICES: AN OVERVIEW

M. Shater Jannati
UNIDO

1. INTRODUCTION

Corruption, the abuse of entrusted power for private gain, is one of the major threats to economic and social development around the world. It creates market distortions, suffocates economic growth, undermines the rule of law and democracy.

There are few other issues which are more cross-cutting and pervasive than corruption, an evil which involves the whole society in all sectors of its activity.

Corruption in the private sector takes many forms, among them bribery, fraud, money laundering and collusion. Generally we can distinguish different categories of business corruption on the basis of its dynamics.

Corruption can take place inside the enterprise: the system of corporate governance is susceptible of abuses. An example can be given by the management focusing on short-term profits, which influence its bonuses, more than on long-term profitability. Conflict of interest, abuses of entrusted power for private gain and other forms of frauds are the most common.

Considering the external relations of a company we can individuate private-to-private and private-to-public corruption. While the latter category clearly includes corrupt practices which involve public officials or civil servants, the former category (also known as commercial bribery) consists of those cases in which the bribe receiver accepts corrupt payments or other favors, in return for making deals that may not be in his or her employer's best interests (Hess, 2009). Such a kind of corruption involves all the value chain of a company and can affect all its business operations, strongly distorting the marketplace. To give some examples, it can affect the employees' hiring process, the choice of suppliers and it is often linked to cartels or collusion of companies.

Whichever the form, corruption has a highly negative impact on the company and on society as a whole, in both developing and developed countries: It fosters a culture and practice of dishonesty; It endangers the basic principles of doing business, fair competition and merit-based selection, which are fundamental for markets to deliver efficiency, innovation and growth; It contributes to environmental damage, health and safety risk, economic instability and human rights violations.

2. INTERNATIONAL LEGAL FRAMEWORK AND GLOBAL INITIATIVES

National governments and international institutions have growingly focused on fighting corruption and, in the last decades, the enforcement of laws targeting corruption in the private sector has raised.

Intergovernmental instruments have been adopted at the international level, with the conclusion of several conventions, such as OECD Convention on Combating Bribery (OECD, 1997) and the United Nations Convention against Corruption (UNODC, 2003).

In the meanwhile, national policies have been implemented, sometimes with global implications for companies, such as in the case of the Foreign Corrupt Practices Act and the Sarbanes-Oxley Act in the US.[48]

It is superficial, however, to think that corruption can be fought only by governments. Some of the major world companies are demonstrating leadership in the field by implementing effective anti-corruption programs within their companies.

---

[48] Foreign Corrupt Practices Act of 1977, as amended, 15 U.S.C. §§ 78dd-1, et seq. ("FCPA"); Sarbanes–Oxley Act of 2002 (Pub.L. 107–204, 116 Stat. 745, enacted July 30, 2002.

Those companies are unable to face alone the multiple challenges created by corrupted systems. Mutually supportive, global, multi-industry initiatives have been launched to address the collective issues which business encounters in combating corruption.

The UN Global Compact, the world largest corporate sustainability initiative, has adopted a 10th Principle against corruption, as a signal that the private sector shares responsibility for combating corruption.

Transparency International has published a code, the "Business Principles for Countering Bribery", with the aim of furnishing a tool for companies to effectively fight against corruption.[49] This code formed the base for the Principles elaborated in the context of the Partnering against Corruption Initiative (PACI) together with the World Economic Forum. PACI is a platform for companies to commit themselves to develop, implement and monitor their anti-corruption policies. Being driven by the private sector, this initiative is an example of the industry effort in fighting corruption and in urging the regulatory framework to do so.

The International Chamber of Commerce, being one of the most authoritative voices of the private sector in the world, has issued the Rules and Recommendations to Combat Extortion and Bribery, promoting the self-regulation of enterprises on the matter and providing an input to companies on how to fight corruption.

Besides those initiatives, Anti-Corruption appears today in the context of the ISO26000, the international standards which identify the core subjects and issues pertaining social responsibility.

3. THE BUSINESS CASE FOR FIGHTING CORRUPTION

Companies are often subject to extortion and some of them play a role in paying bribes. The private sector, thus, is a part of the problem and, accordingly, it has to be a part of the solution.

The question which has often been posed is whether or not a business case for countering corruption exists. The business case is clear.

Corruption makes business more expensive by imposing extraordinary expenses and obstacles to grow. Estimates show that corruption "adds up to 10 per cent to the total cost of doing business globally, and up to 25 percent to the

---

[49] The latest version was published in 2013 and it is available at: http://www.transparency.org /whatwedo/pub/business_principles_for_countering_bribery (latest accessed on 1st October 2014).

cost of public procurement contracts in developing countries" (World Economic Forum, 2008).

Moving business from a country where the level of corruption is low to a highly corrupted country is found to correspond to a 20 per cent tax on foreign business (World Economic Forum, 2008).

Adopting bribing practices, moreover, means taking a so-called "casino risk", as a reliable assurance that the counterpart will deliver (or that it will not change the conditions of the agreement, e.g. by increasing the price) is never given and no legal remedies exists in such a case, due to the criminal nature of the agreement.

In addition to direct financial cost (and lost business opportunities), corruption in the private sector has even higher indirect costs.

First, engaging in corrupt practices implies incurring in a high reputational risk. The global public is increasingly requiring transparency, accountability and integrity in business. Involvement in corruption can produce deep damages to companies' reputation, which can dramatically affect the value of a company's brand and its external business relationship, as well as government relations.

Moreover, engaging in corruption is time and resource consuming: Companies need to spend time and resources to deal with corrupt practices and avoiding the legal consequences of such practices.

Legal liability, as a consequence of engaging in corrupt practices, strengthens the business case for countering corruption. This holds true especially in light of the severe enforcement of anti-bribery laws in some jurisdictions.

On the other hand, responsible practices also pay direct rewards. Good business offers brand and marketing opportunities that can increase the volume of sales in sectors sensitive to consumer perceptions and promote longer and stable relations with costumers, in light of the said growing demand for integrity and transparency of the public opinion. For the same reason, companies engaging in the anti-corruption fight are more attractive to investment from ethically oriented investors and to highly principled employees, whose morale is proved to be improved in a clean business context.

The business case for engaging in combating corruption is stronger if, apart from the individual action of companies, we take into consideration the collective action of the private sector. Private concerted practices have several benefits: the reduction of market distortions and the creation of a level playing field which overcomes the prisoner's dilemma; the improvement of public trust in business and the possibility to positively influence future laws and regulations.

4. MNCS AND CORRUPTION IN DEVELOPING COUNTRIES

Corruption risk is particularly high for those companies doing business in developing economies, where a high corruption level is registered. Corrupt practices in those countries have devastating effects, undermining development and exacerbate inequality and poverty (Hawley, 2001).

MNCs' supply chains in developing areas mainly consist of small and medium local enterprises. Local businesses often lack global perspective and have less discomfort with participating in corruption, especially in those cultures where it is the norm. Small enterprises, on the other side, can lack the leverage to resist corruption and influence local institutions.

MNCs can, thus, have a positive impact on business integrity in those economies, especially in the light of the increasing shift of global manufacturing towards developing countries.

MNCs usually lead global supply chains and, in order to secure the efficiency of those chains, have to establish close relationships with suppliers and are deeply involved in organizational and planning aspects. This implies that the responsibility of supply chain leaders to respect standards of corporate integrity also applies to the wider supply chain.

Aligning corporate governance and practices with company values and principles of corporate integrity is more difficult when the institutional government is weak. Inefficient institutions not only fail to provide the necessary guidance for responsible corporate behavior, but usually undermine it. Weak institutions are often synonym of poor protection of land property rights and human rights, arbitrary enforcement of regulation, high level of corruption.

As a consequence, companies may tend to adopt bribery or other corrupt practices to avoid the obstacles created by the political and institutional context and protect their investment. Corruption can be used at high levels to influence the political, regulatory or legislative decisions, but bribing is often seen as a means to speed up day-to-day administrative processes and secure or expedite the performance of a necessary action by the local bureaucracy, as well as a tool to obtain licenses.

It is evident that the use of those practices mainly reinforces the existing system, increasing market uncertainty by undermining fair competition and the predictability of regulations. Companies linking themselves to corrupted governments, not only risk enormous reputational damages, but also run the risk of tying their investment to the fate of a specific political party or broker.

In such an environment, companies should have a specific anti-corruption strategy. Awareness is important. Mapping the risk and building a tailored compliance and anti-corruption program ensure clear rules and procedures on how to react to corruption demands.

The positive impact that MNCs can have on the fight against corrupt practices in developing countries, however, is not automatic. Compliance efforts must be strong and really integrated throughout the supply chain to avoid a magnification of the problem.

5. GLOBAL ANTI-CORRUPTION PROGRAMS AND THE SUPPLY CHAIN

As a consequence of the increasing awareness on corruption issues among civil society, in the governments' agendas and in the public opinion, spurred also by some of the big scandals that have interested the corporate world in the last decade, bribery and corruption are gaining a bigger space in Corporate Social Responsibility (CSR) policies.

Anti-Corruption efforts are, thus, becoming more and more important in the action of companies to act as responsible citizens and to respond to the expectations of society, even though other fields of action, as environmental protection and human rights, are still considered to be the priority in the CSR agenda.

As said in the previous paragraph, the effectiveness of a company's anti-corruption engagement depends on the implementation of a tailored anti-corruption program and its integration throughout all levels of the corporate structure. Implementing an effective program, thus, requires constant efforts and a context-specific approach.

Bearing what said in mind, a number of companies have adopted different programs. Some common elements have been identified by Transparency International: in 2005 the organisation elaborated a Six-Step Process for the development of an effective anti-corruption program, which complemented the already existing Business Pricinples for Countering Bribery, in the effort to provide the private sector with a toolkit against corruption (Transparency International, 2005).

As to develop an effective anti-corruption action, a company has, first of all, to articulate a policy which promotes zero tolerance for corrupt practices. The said policy has then to be implemented through a detailed program, which ensures employees awareness throughout the organizational structure of the company and trains them to respond properly to corruption risks.

The effectiveness of the program passes through another element: the top-level commitment to anti-corruption. Corporate efforts to fight corruption can be successful only when the high-level management and the board of directors of a company are strongly committed to high performance and high integrity. The latter counts three components: adherence to the spirit of rules, the voluntary adoption of global ethics standards which bind the whole company and its staff; employees commitment to core values such as honesty, fairness, reliability (Heineman, 2009).

It is the top management, thus, that has to foster the culture of "high performance with high integrity", which is the prerequisite for the effectiveness of an anti-corruption program (Heineman, 2009).

This implies that all aspects of the company activity should reflect the commitment of the firm to zero tolerance and high integrity. Selection and recruitment of personnel, promotion schemes and all other aspects of human resource management should be based on rewarding integrity and sanctioning deviated actions. The same holds true for communication and reporting policies: employees should have secure channels to report violations and concerns, and should be able to express their questions and doubts on the implementation of the program. Accounting and record keeping should follow the same path: the reliability of financial records and a good system of internal controls are of utmost importance in the fight against corruption, given the fact that bribes are often paid with the use of secret reserves or "slush funds" (Coté-Freeman, 2008).

A program of the said kind is meant to address the risks which are specific to the company it has been created for, protecting it from corruption. However, this is only the first step towards an effective anti-corruption action: a company must ensure that business partners, suppliers, subsidiaries, agents and contractors are carefully selected, according to the principles of its zero tolerance policy. Once again the action of a company cannot stop at its doors.

While in the past, integrity in the supply chain was ensured mainly by the use of monitoring and audit tools and focused on labor and environmental issues, today this control-based approached is not enough. Addressing the new issues brought about by global supply chains requires the players of the chain to cooperate and operate as partners, by sharing information and improving the level of dialogue between companies.

Four pillars have been identified as fundamental to make supply chains effective and sustainable: the internal alignment between commercial and social objectives; the supplier ownership of labor and environmental conditions; the empowerment of workers and; public policy frameworks that foster public-private dialogue, partnership and solutions (Business for Social Responsibility, 2007).

6. COLLECTIVE ACTION

Individual initiatives through anti-corruption programs and policies are necessary, but the effectiveness of the fight against corruption is enhanced by collective action, which fosters a fairly competitive market and strengthens the influence of the private sector in eradicating corruption.

Collective action can work through different mechanisms: integrity pacts for bidding and executing public contracts; application of code of conducts to all public tenders; collaboration to ensure transparency in the sector of activity; the establishment of common rules on business relations with national and local governments; identification of key priorities for action and adoption of a single voice on anti-corruption policies in the relations with the public sector; creation of platforms for discussion and for sharing sensitive information; concerted training and creation of expertise on anti-corruption action.

Whichever the mechanism adopted, some characteristics seem to be fundamental for the success of the action. Firstly, the presence of external facilitation seems to be of the greatest importance: an intermediary organization, acting as a convener or facilitator, simplifies the functioning of collective initiatives, by providing "coordinating energy". (Brew and Moberg, 2006)

Secondly, collective action requires a collective approach: the traditional corporate culture and the managerial procedures which lead to unilateral action are to be combined with practice norms agreed on as part of a concerted effort.

Finally, collective action has to have a local component. Global initiatives are extremely important and play a big role in the fight against corruption. Those initiatives, however, are meant to work as a support mechanism which provides a framework for action, a valuable foundation on which to build sectoral and local initiatives.

CONCLUSION

Corruption threats both developed and developing countries and it affects all aspect of a society, hindering its economic and social development.

Governments, business and civil society are all responsible for combating corruption. Apart from moral and societal interests and reasons, companies have to actively fight corruption to protect the efficiency and the effectiveness of their operations, as well as the functioning and the growth of a fair and competitive market.

It is, thus, necessary that enterprises step forwards and take their part in the fight against corruption. Each enterprise individually and the business sector as a whole have the responsibility to do so. The active involvement of the business community in combating corruption is essential for meeting local and global governance challenges. Some of the most important public policy issues that the world faces today can be effectively tackled only if the private sector, civil society and governments act together and in the same direction. Effective regulations must be complemented by effective implementation and supported by a transparent private sector, accountable for its actions to a public opinion which has to be demanding and participative.

In this context, MNCs play an important role, having the responsibility to promote integrity and fight corruption along their supply chain, especially in those countries where governments are weak and corruption is the rule.

Zero tolerance policies, anti-corruption programs, codes of conduct are the instruments to be used to create the culture of integrity necessary to eradicate corruption, but individual action is to be supported by collective action. Acting together reinforces and enhances the impact of the individual efforts of each company, improving the environment in which enterprises work and strengthen their influence in reducing corruption within and outside their sector of operation.

REFERENCES

Barenblat, A., & Rangarajan, T. (2009). *Strengthening compliance and integrity in the supply chain: what comes next?*. Global Corruption Report 2009, Corruption and the Private Sector, Cambridge Universtity Press.

Boehm, F., & Huber-Grabenwarter, G. (2009). *Laying the foundations for sound and sustainable development: strengthening corporate integrity in weak governance zones.* Global Corruption Report 2009, Corruption and the Private Sector, Cambridge Universtity Press.

Brew, P., & Moberg, J. (2006). *The power of joining forces - The case for collective action in fighting corruption.* Business Against Corruption, United Nations Global Compact Office.

Hardoon, D., & Heinrich, F. (2011). *Bribe Payers Index 2011,* Transparency International.

Heineman, B.W. Jr. (2009). *View from the inside – Robust anti-corruption programmes in a high-performance with high integrity global company.* Global Corruption Report 2009, Corruption and the Private Sector, Cambridge Universtity Press.

Hess, D. (2009). *Corruption in the value chain: private-to-private and private-to-public corruption.* Global Corruption Report 2009, Corruption and the Private Sector, Cambridge Universtity Press.

Mendez Indrighi, D. (2009). *Corruption inside the enterprise: corporate fraud and conflicts of interest.* Global Corruption Report 2009, Corruption and the Private Sector, Cambridge Universtity Press.

OECD (1997). *Convention on Combating Bribery of Foreign Public Officials in International Business Transactions,* available at: http://www.oecd.org/daf/anti-bribery/ConvCombatBribery_ENG.pdf (latest accessed: 1st October 2014)

Sullivan, J. (2006). *Corruption, economic development and governance: Private sector perspectives from developing countries.* Business Against Corruption, United Nations Global Compact Office.

Transparency International (2005). *Business Principles for Countering Bribery: TI Six Step Process. A practical guide for companies implementing anti-bribery policies and Programme.* Available at: http://archive.transparency.org/global_priorities/private_sector/business_p rinciples/six_step_implementation_process (latest accessed: 1st October 2014)

Transparency International (2009). *The scale and challenge of private sector corruption.* Global Corruption Report 2009, Corruption and the Private Sector, Cambridge Universtity Press.

United Nations Office on Drugs and Crime (2003). *United Nations Convention against Corruption.* Available at: https://www.unodc.org/documents /treaties/UNCAC/Publications/Convention/08-50026_E.pdf (latest accessed: 1st October 2014)

Vincke, F. (2006). *Anti-corruption: A business case?.* Business Against Corruption, United Nations Global Compact Office.

In: Multinational's CSR Practices …   ISBN: 978-1-63463-479-3
Editor: Alidou Ouedraogo   © 2015 Nova Science Publishers, Inc.

Chapter 4

THE BUSINESS CASE CSR FOR THE WORLD MARKET LEADER IN BRICK PRODUCTION (WIENERBERGER TUMKUR SITE – INDIA)

M. Neureiter
The CSR Company International, Vienna, Austria

Wienerberger is the world largest brick producer, present in 27 countries in the world. One of them is India, the first developing country Wienerberger is active in.

When the decision was taken to enter the Indian market in 2006 it was not quite clear how this would happen. First option was to work this country the same as all the others the company was active in, meaning, concentrating on the technical and commercial aspects and trying to keep within the legal framework of the host country.

It was the newly designated country manager for India, an Austrian expat with several years of experience in India, who came up with the idea that it would be necessary to include a strong CSR component into the market entry strategy, as this market was significantly different than all the other markets in which Wienerberger was active.

For that purpose he researched the market for CSR advisors with an international component to them and came across the CSR Company International, a Vienna based company with offices in 14 different countries and a number of large and medium sized clients.

But that alone did not do the trick. The CEO had to be convinced. And that turned out to be a tough call. In a first reaction to the country manager he told him, CSR is a waste of money and that the company would do in India just as it had so successfully entered all the other markets. It was thanks to the persistence of the country manager who insisted that without this CSR component the risk of failure was great and that would mean loss of money in a much larger dimension than what would be put aside for CSR.

Finally, after several months, the CEO agreed to hold a meeting at his office to discuss this issue. So we came to corporate headquarters in Vienna, a 34 story high glass tower in the south of the city overlooking the town on the one side and the flat lands out to the south on the other. His office was of course on the top floor with a beautiful view and the day was sunny with clear skies, so the horizon was far away.

We started the discussion and we tried to explain our approach to CSR as a strategic approach serving the business needs and engaging the stakeholders and taking into account their expectations. So we started to brainstorm what we could be doing for the people living in Tumkur around our proposed factory site.

As we are polite people, we had the CEO have the first idea. He came up with the grand idea that we could support saving the tigers in India, they are an endangered species and the attention in Europe for these wild cats is big. It was on me to say something to this, as everybody looked at me waiting for what I would say to this proposal. That is the job of a third party person in such meetings. So I started by saying that generally that was a good idea but what was the connection between tigers and bricks? Maybe only the colour is similar, everything else does not fit. The tigers live approximately 2000 kilometres further north than where our site was, they are in India by far not as popular consdiering they kill farm animals and sometimes the farmer himself, and they live in protected areas which cannot be used for farming, so their image is a very different one than from a European perspective.

So from our perspective in the comfortable leather office chairs overlooking Vienna we tried to decide what would be good for people living in rural India, near our site and know what their needs and expectations would be.

My suggestion then was, what we actually need to know is whom are we dealing with, who are our neighbours, what are they, what is their education, their income situation, their expectations etc. Only then it would make sense to set the agenda and decide what we could contribute.

And so it was done. We hired students from the University of Bangalore, the sociology faculty, to do a household survey. For that purpose we simply drew a circle of 10 kilometres around our plant and declared it our impact zone. It could just the same have been 8 kilometres or 12, there was no magic to that figure, it just seemed the obvious one.

The students knocked on every door and asked how many people lived in the household, how many men, women, children, what education the people had, which religion they belonged to, which caste, what they did for a living, their age etc. and all the basic data we needed to know. But that was not all: We also asked what their greatest needs were. That was a crucial question as we should learn later.

We learned that we had around 2900 people living in the immediate surroundings of our plant, 90% of them day labour workers, some land owners and some skilled labour. They are mainly Hindu, some are Muslims and some belong to different sects. There are two predominating castes. No child has made it further than basic education.

On the needs there were three clear priorities. Number one was jobs: Being day labourers they wanted permanent jobs. The average income is around 1.5 Dollars a day per person, but nothing during Monsoon time or when sick etc.

Now this is a difficult thing for a brick producer. Normally in India maybe not, but for this particular one it is. In India brick production is a low tech business. Many brick producers are very local, in the village, digging out clay and putting it into the sun to dry and that is the brick. Of course there are also more sophisticated production sites, but none that could compete with this factory. Just to give the reader an idea of this factory, it is the largest brick producing factory in India, but not only that, it is the largest in all of Asia. It has a daily production amount of 35.000 bricks and it still has the option to double this output. It is a one to one model of a factory built by Wienerberger in Belgium, so it also complies with EU environmental standards although standing in the middle of rural India. The reason for that is not necessarily the commitment of Wienerberger to comply with EU regulations in India but the simple fact that it is cheaper to rebuild an existing factory and all its processes than having to adjust the processes newly to a new set of production line. Anyhow it took Wienerberger a lot longer to get the factory started than initially planned, but for many different reasons.

But what has that to do with job creation? It sounds like a lot of jobs. An Indian factory of this size would have to employ 1000s of workers, actually around 15.000 to be exact. And how many does this factory need? 28 workers and no more. And not unskilled labour, but highly skilled comsputer experts who are trained for 9 months in Austria on the machines. So this factory is not a job creation exercise. On the first expectation we would not be able to deliver. Nevertheless, we tried something by promising that every family who lost a piece of land because of our factory, at least one member would get a job. This would be as driver, gardener or security guard. But even that took us more than a year to accomplish. And these are just a handful of jobs.

The second need expressed was health. Based on the fact of malnutrition – the basic food of the people is based on 4-5 crops grown – they develop mainly diabetes and some eye diseases, some coming from diabetes, some from the flies and other hygienic defaults. So a lot of elder people get blind, which stops them from working and they become a burden for the families, another mouth to be fed.

Now a brick company is not a health care provider, so we were thinking hard what we can do on this expectation. We learned that there are state run health care centres in some villages around our plant. So we visited the one closest to the factory. The surprise was great, we found it, we entered, and stood in an empty room. A friendly man told us, yes, this is the rural health centre, they have no furniture and no apparatuses and no medicine, but people come here and a trained person looks at them and tells them what they should be doing.

Driving back from there we decided we would build a proper health station in the nearest village and set up a proper structure to provide people with the necessary health support. But that should take time; we first needed to find a piece of land in a good location in the village. Finally we got one. But before that building was going to go up we wanted to do something immediately. We decided that, based on the research done by the students of Bangalore Sociology faculty, we would look into eyesight. We came up with the idea of an Eyecamp.

The Eyecamp: It was set up as a one day activity; we invited all the people living around the factory to come to the school on a certain date. We got some eye doctors from Bangalore to do tests on the people for their eyesight. We had the employees of the factory use the day as a volunteering activity for the community. More than 500 people came. It was a huge success. Around 70 people got glasses prescribed and Wienerberger took the costs for them and another 60 people needed an eye operation to recover eyesight, they had gone blind already. Such an operation is not a big deal moneywise, they cost around 100 dollars each, but for people earning 1,5 dollars a day that is big money. So the company also covered this cost. It should later prove to be one of our best investments – but read about that later.

Concerning the health centre, do not expect that this is a huge building; it is actually a 5meters x 4 meters building with two rooms, built with Wienerberger bricks. Also this should have an unexpected effect, but also that a little bit later. The first issue was: We have a building, but what now? We are a brick company, not a health care provider. We do not have any experience in this, nor do we want any as it is not our core business. So we looked for a partner who would actually run the centre. We came across the Karuna Trust, an NGO that runs 100s of these centres all over India, mainly in very remote areas, with great success. The founder even won the Alternative Nobel Prize for his engagement. They agreed and took over the management of the centre, while we paid for a nurse that would be there every day in the morning and a visiting doctor who would come once a week for more serious cases. We also pay for the equipment and the medicine. The centre is a full success story, also for one other reason, which links this activity to business. The house is built with Wienerberger bricks which insulate much better than classical Indian bricks as they have a hollow structure inside, so the people noticed that inside the building there is a much better climate than outside and they can touch the bricks without a salesperson coming to them and asking if they can help them. The building is in the middle of the village so every passer-by can knock on them, see and feel the difference and get a first impression. And to make a long story short, in a radius of 30 kilometers there is no local brick producer anymore, because people only want to buy our brick, as they can experience the difference.

After we got this health centre up and running the CEO in Vienna was still very sceptical about the whole exercise, he still thought it was just a waste of money. We could do without it and save the money. Maybe here is in the right place to mention that for all the CSR activities including our services there was only a budget of 25.000 Euros allocated. That included all activities like building the health centre, the Eyecamp and our consulting fees. A joke of a budget in comparison to the costs of setting up the factory there, but the best we could get at the time. And why did we agree as a consulting company to such a contract? Well, first it is about getting the foot in the door, secondly it is a well known multinational company, so it makes itself good on the reference list and thirdly we really believe in what we are doing, so we are sure we will convince them of our work and get a better deal next time round.

And it did not take long until this opportunity came along. India is a big democracy, of which it can be very proud of. But democracy is also expensive.

So one nice day a candidate for one party came to the factory and talked with management and mentioned that he would like to have one million Dollars from the company to support his campaign. He would act favourably for the company and support us whenever and in whatever once elected. The company called also me and asked what to do and my answer was a clear "no," do not pay. Maybe he wins this time, but next time around the other party will win and then you are stamped as a supporter of that party that lost and will have a rough time, or they will want you also to pay a million dollars to support them. Better not to pay.

This guy did not take that message too good. He organised some 100 people to demonstrate in front of our factory, block the entrance, throw stones at the trucks trying to pass and in general halting the activities at the gate, which would make the production stop if lasting for a longer time. Actually a few days would be enough. And then something astonishing happened. The people from the nearby village came and threw the demonstrators out, telling them that this is a good company, they want us to be here, some of the people who came were the ones who had their eyesight given back by the operation we had financed. We did not have to call the police, not our own security guards; it was the people of the village who saved us from a delicate situation. What more can you ask for as being an accepted part of the local society? When we reported this to the CEO back in Vienna he gave us all 27 countries to do the CSR work because finally he realised the connection between doing CSR and money. It would have cost us 1000s of dollars if we would have had to close production for several days, but the people of the village prevented that because of our previous actions.

Just imagine if we would have followed the initial idea of supporting the tigers.

In: Multinational's CSR Practices ...   ISBN: 978-1-63463-479-3
Editor: Alidou Ouedraogo   © 2015 Nova Science Publishers, Inc.

Chapter 5

THE NEED FOR A FINER GRAINED ANALYSIS OF THE CSR OF MNC SUBSIDIARIES IN DEVELOPING COUNTRIES

D. Jamali

Olayan School of Business,
American University of Beirut, Beirut, Lebanon

INTRODUCTION

Multinational Corporations (MNCs) have been growing and expanding in their reach and influence, transcending geographic boundaries and economic divides, and turning into very powerful agents, economically and socially (Jamali and Mirshak, 2010). They have grown so powerful that the revenues of some of the larger MNCs often exceed the GDP of some developing states in which they operate (Chandler and Mazlish, 2005). Their power increases not only with the amount of resources they control but also with their mobility and capacity of shifting resources to match their demands on increasing profits (Scherer and Palazzo, 2008). MNCs are one of the key drivers of globalization and due to their operations across multiple legal and political systems, governments find themselves weakened and their regulatory power contracted vis-à-vis MNC activities (Scherer and Palazzo, 2008).

However, globalization, deregulation and privatization, accompanied with the emergence of global risks, seem to have re-directed attention to MNCs in recent years and the positive and negative consequences of their global operations in general (Korten, 2001; Strike et al., 2006), and their Corporate Social Responsibility (CSR) activities in developing countries more specifically (Ite, 2004; Mohan, 2006; Scherer and Palazzo, 2008).

Within the larger debate on the merits and evils of globalization, MNCs and their CSR interventions have received mixed characterizations; some scholars highlight the negative spillover effects of MNC intrusions in developing countries (Jones et al., 2005; Donaldson, 2001) while others argue that global and institutional pressures are catalyzing higher levels of CSR involvement by MNCs, and improvement in social and environmental conditions (Bansal and Roth, 2000; Chirstmann, 2004).

Generally, however the literature tends to suggest that MNCs have encouraged a race to the bottom in developing countries, with more critical voices echoed about the global risks associated with their operations, such as corruption and human rights abuses, problems that often exceed the monitoring and regulatory capacity of local communities and national governments (Scherer and Palazzo, 2008). Therefore, the debate over MNC-CSR involvement in developing countries has been extremely polarized in recent years (Jamali, 2010), with Kolk and van Tulder (2006) claiming that it has been overall difficult to assess the direct and indirect effects of MNCs'-CSR activities in developing countries.

In this book chapter, the discussion about different ways MNCs can approach CSR in developing countries is revisited, especially global standardized approaches versus localized CSR interventions. In this respect, while some authors claim that MNCs can improve the effectiveness of their CSR through more systematic stakeholder engagement and local tailoring, the book chapter highlights the practical challenges associated with enacting localized and tailored CSR strategies that address local community needs.

For different reasons, developing country contexts often do not provide conducive environments for investing in CSR initiatives that are substantive or tailored to local specificities.

From there, the book chapter will refocus the discussion on the importance of context and how different institutional constellations in general, and developing country institutional constellations more specifically invariably affect the design, enactment, and outcomes of CSR activities.

The specific institutional constellations of developing countries also help account for the continuing difficulties in assessing precisely the CSR track record of MNCs in developing countries.

1. THEMES OF GLOBAL VERSUS LOCAL CSR FOR MNCS

Difficulties associated with the assessment of the track record of MNC-CSR involvement in developing countries are no doubt related to the vagueness of the concept of CSR itself which remains highly elusive and contested (Matten and Moon, 2008). They are also in no small part related to the complexities of MNCs which are often networks of heterogeneous and loosely connected subsidiaries engaged in multi-faceted activities within and between many host countries (Strike et al., 2006; Blumentritt and Nigh, 2002). MNCs are in fact not singular organizations, but sets of differentiated entities and processes, and their subsidiaries may exhibit significant diversity in strategy and structure (Blumentritt and Nigh, 2002; Rosenzweig and Singh, 1991; Jamali and Mirshak, 2010).

When developing their CSR strategies, MNCs can either adopt CSR practices of their home country which is known by global CSR or tailor their CSR practices to the context of their host country which is called local CSR (Muller, 2006). Muller (2006) aptly recognizes in this respect that issues of local responsiveness *vs.* global integration have received considerable attention in the international management literature, yet they have not been accorded systematic attention in relation to CSR. Perspectives differ on whether MNCs should stimulate centralized CSR strategies or whether they should develop those locally in consultation with local stakeholders (Muller, 2006). Table I makes clear that each of these strategies presents distinct advantages and disadvantages. While global strategies may be more proactive, efficient, and integrated, they often lack ownership and legitimacy at the local level; decentralized strategies on the other hand while locally responsive may be fragmented and ad hoc (Jamali, 2010).

Husted and Allen (2006) suggest that the key difference between global and local CSR is the community that demands it. Local CSR deals with the firm's obligations based on the standards of the local community whereas global CSR deals with the firm's obligations based on hyper norms or standards of the global company or home country (Husted and Allen, 2006). Research to date seems to suggest that the majority of MNCs evolve generic themes and strategies for their CSR across countries focusing on education, healthcare, and the environment or a combination thereof (Kolk and Lenfant, 2010). Jamali (2010) reports that the CSR strategies of MNC subsidiaries in developing countries are enacted using the same global themes, but are often more diluted depending on the nature of the specific market environment encountered (Jamali, 2010).

Table 1. Global *vs.* Local CSR in MNCs

	Advantages	Disadvantages
Global CSR	– Upward harmonization of CSR standards internationally – Globally integrated and standardised strategy – Policies, processes and structures consistent across cultures	– Insensitivity to local needs – Reduced ownership and legitimacy – Compliance based strategies that are tailored to end of pipe controls – Approaches that live up to minimum host requirements
Local CSR	– Nationally responsive and adapted to local context – Tailored to local cultural differences and preferences	– Fragmented inconsistent and reactive strategies – Lack of clear responsibility and internal tensions – Approaches that live up to minimum global requirements – High coordination and control necessary

Adapted from Jamali, 2010.

Very few MNCs focus on the social issues that are most relevant and endemic in the developing world including institution building, human rights, anti-corruption efforts and poverty alleviation (Jamali and Mirshak, 2010). For example, in the majority, MNCs remain silent about conflict issues, although conflict is pervasive and endemic in developing countries (Kolk and Lenfant, 2010). Generally, the literature seems to suggest that MNCs fail to effectively address matters of key importance in their host countries (Logsdon and Wood, 2005). Amaeshi and Amao (2009) in their research on MNCs operating in Nigeria concluded that the codes of conduct adopted by MNCs are influenced by the characteristics of their home countries; more specifically, codes of conduct reflect their home countries' models of capitalism. Findings from the Lebanese context similarly reveal that CSR initiatives designed by MNC subsidiaries were inspired and guided by global directives suggesting that MNCs are not according systematic attention to the priorities of their local stakeholders nor actually involving them in the decision-making process (Jamali, 2010). This is despite evidence from Mexico that decentralized decision-making is linked to higher local CSR performance in 'low-CSR countries' or, in other words, developing countries.

So although local CSR strategies may be more conducive to meeting needs and expectations in local contexts, few MNCs manage to actually implement those wholeheartedly and effectively, particularly in the developing world.

2. CHALLENGES FACING LOCALIZED CSR STRATEGIES BY MNCS

Undeniably, MNC subsidiaries face a wide range of potential risks and challenges in developing countries especially when it comes to aligning their CSR approach with local norms and expectations. The major local challenges that MNCs encounter and that are mostly specific to the markets in developing countries are poverty, inequality, unemployment and environmental concerns, undemocratic political institutions and dysfunctional institutions in general (Newenham-Kahindi, 2011; Ite, 2004).

Cruz and Boehe (2010) identified specific challenges in designing CSR initiatives in developing countries, such as building competitive advantages based on CSR, local adaptation by responding to local stakeholders' issues in the host country and global learning. According to the authors, the more diverse the challenges will become, the more disintegrated CSR will be and this will make it more difficult to learn from fragmented and diverse local experiences (Cruz and Boehe, 2010). In addition, coordinating, integrating and exchanging knowledge, information and resources are major challenges faced by MNC subsidiaries that are geographically dispersed (Jamali, 2010; Strike et al., 2006). Sometimes, limited budgetary allocations and centralized decision-making reflect in the adoption of generic philanthropic CSR gestures by MNC subsidiaries that are detached from the realities of the local context (Jamali and Neville, 2011).

One of the most critical issues that MNCs face relates to establishing and maintaining legitimacy in various host countries (Kostova and Roth, 2002; Kostova and Zaheer, 1999). Legitimacy in fact constitutes a key mechanism of social control in relation to CSR (Bitektine, 2011) in developing countries. By conferring legitimacy on organizations, social actors provide them with a license to continue to operate and grow. Suchman (1995, p. 574) defines legitimacy as "a generalized perception or assumption that the actions of an entity are desirable, proper or appropriate, within some socially constructed system of norms, values, beliefs and definitions."

But legitimacy itself is a complex concept, and various legitimacy typologies have been identified in the literature (Bitektine, 2011), including pragmatic legitimacy (based on self-interested calculations), moral legitimacy (based on normative approval), cognitive legitimacy (based on rational reasoning and cognitive templates), internal legitimacy (based on internal views and considerations) and external legitimacy (based on the views of external stakeholders and constituencies). Legitimacy is therefore a complex and multi-faceted concept and the maintenance of legitimacy in multiple host environments is one of the most critical challenges facing MNCs (Kostova and Roth, 2002; Kostova and Zaheer, 1999).

In fact, for MNCs that operate in different countries across the globe, legitimacy is not only affected by the number of countries in which an MNC operates but also by the extent of variety or differences across these countries (Kostova and Zaheer, 1999). Some authors recognize that multiple legitimacy considerations influence MNC decisions and identify what is referred to as "institutional duality" which is the pressure to conform to both the parent company (home country institutional pressures) and to isomorphic pressures specific to the host country (Kostova and Roth, 2002; Hillman and Wan, 2005). One of the most difficult challenges facing MNCs and their subsidiaries in this regard stems from the fact that judgment as to whether an organization and its actions are perceived as legitimate is socially constructed and hence context dependent. In other words, MNCs cannot invoke and leverage a universal legitimacy model, and may experience discrepancies in judgments over the nature of legitimacy between home country and host country environments (Barkemeyer, 2007). There is thus a real danger when the CSR activities of MNC subsidiaries are detached from local contextual priorities, which often leads to the preponderance of symbolic (versus substantive) legitimacy management in the developing world, and the misallocation of resources where they are most needed.

3. HOW INSTITUTIONS AFFECT THE DESIGN, ENACTMENT AND OUTCOME OF CSR ACTIVITIES

As fleshed out above, MNCs face multiple institutional environments specific to each country they operate in as part of their growth and expansion process. Institutional environments are forces that exert pressure on firms based on the specific features and constellations of the economic political and societal context (Boxenbaum, 2006). The reality is that MNC CSR strategies cannot be detached from context, and the CSR practice of MNC subsidiaries in the developing world is invariably affected by variance in legal regimes, institutional structure, social and cultural attitudes, natural endowment of production factors and environmental conditions (Ite, 2005; Jamali and Neville, 2011). MNC efforts in the developing world are also invariably affected by the strength of the pressure felt and exerted by various institutional groups, including governmental entities, business associations, non-governmental organizations, communities in which MNCs operate, and consumers in general (Yang and Rivers, 2009).

So on one hand, as global corporations are expanding and their visibility is increasing, they are facing escalating pressure for CSR in their operations, especially in developing countries (Scherer and Palazzo, 2008). On the other hand, it is important to remember that in such environments, institutions are largely dysfunctional, with lax regulations, weak legal and judicial enforcement, thus creating room for abuses of human rights and corruption among others. These abuses may serve in turn to reinforce and exacerbate a mode of non-responsible involvement in the developing world and worsen existing cycles of poverty (Khavul and Bruton, 2013; Newenham-Kahindi, 2011). Governments, in their attempt to attract foreign investment may also turn a blind eye or ignore irresponsible behavior and refuse to set regulations and enforce protective standards (Aman, 2001). This is one scenario that should be kept in mind when considering MNCs and CSR interventions in developing countries. According to Ite (2004), lack of national management and planning along with an inequitable resource allocation and the absence of an enabling environment have significant implications for CSR performance and the sustainability of CSR initiatives of MNCs in developing countries.

The reality is that even in the absence of governmental protection, MNCs are expected to act ethically and responsibly in accordance with the spirit and stipulations of their CSR guidelines and codes of conduct in both developed and developing countries (Matten and Crane, 2005; Eweje, 2006). According to Ite (2005), corruption, poor governance and lack of accountability and transparency have led to relying heavily on the good faith and self-regulatory practices of MNCs. But many MNCs are signatories of global accountability standards like the UN Global Compact and expected to comply with their basic responsibility principles across borders (Jamali, 2010b). CSR in fact does not stop at a nation's borders. It could even be argued that MNCs should be held morally accountable for their behaviors and actions in developing countries, and expected to conform to even higher and more stringent levels and standards of CSR, given the chronic institutional deficits, and exponential social needs encountered across the developing world. The problem however is that it is very difficult to track and manage the activities of MNCs and ensure that their behavior in practice is consistent with their CSR rhetoric, particularly in developing countries where institutional voids are aggravated.

CONCLUSION AND FUTURE RESEARCH

The complexities highlighted in this book chapter help account for the lingering controversy over the track record of MNCs CSR interventions in developing countries. They also highlight the critical need for more research on the topic. Specifically, research should flesh out how the institutional environments of developing countries affect the CSR activities of MNCs and what MNCs can do to mitigate potential negative influences. A finer grained analysis and research agenda is needed to assess the comparative advantages of global or centralized versus local / decentralized CSR strategies for MNCs when entering markets in developing countries. Centralized strategies may be more efficient, but are not necessarily effective in tailoring to local needs. Given that legitimacy is context dependent and socially constructed as highlighted above, it is not recommended for MNCs to adopt global CSR strategies, but rather to seek the increased integration of local stakeholders in CSR agenda setting processes and identifying priorities that match local conceptions of legitimacy and effectiveness.

The other question that certainly deserves more attention in future research about the topic relates to the extent that MNCs can be allowed to abuse the existing global legal vacuum in relation to their business and CSR activities in the developing world. Because of institutional voids prevalent across the developing world, there are significant risks of accountability gaps coupled with institutional voids and legal abstraction in the context of largely self-regulatory CSR initiatives (Willke and Willke, 2008; Jenkins, 2005). MNCs therefore have ample opportunities to evade calls for accountability in this transnational space, and focus on symbolic impression management, as opposed to substantive CSR engagement. However, a common argument in the CSR debate that should be emphasized and invoked in relation to MNCs is the fact that larger firms should be held to higher CSR standards in the developing world, owing to their influence and visibility. Developing country stakeholders should therefore be more careful and exercise significant scrutiny as they confer legitimacy on the CSR of MNCs given that it constitutes the most important mechanism of social control they have at their disposal.

REFERENCES

Amaeshi, K. and Amao, O. (2009). Corporate Social Responsibility in Transnational Spaces: Exploring Influences of Varieties of Capitalism on Expressions of Corporate Codes of Conduct in Nigeria. *Journal of Business Ethics*, Vol. 86, pp. 225-239.

Aman, Jr. (2001). Privatization and the Democracy Problem in Globalization: Making Markets More Accountable through Administrative Law. *Fordham Urban Law Journal*, Vol. 28, pp. 1477-1506.

Bansal, P. and Roth, K. (2000). Why Companies Go Green: A Model of Ecological Responsiveness. *Academy of Management Journal*, Vol. 43, pp. 717-737.

Barkemeyer, R. (2007). Legitimacy as a Key Driver and Determinant of CSR in Developing Countries. *Paper for the 2007 Marie Curie Summer School on Earth System Governance*, University of St. Andrews and Sustainable Development Research Centre (SDRC) School of Management.

Bitektine, A. (2011). Toward a Theory of Social Judgments of Organizations: The Case of Legitimacy, Reputation and Status. *Academy of Management Review*, Vol. 36, No. 1, pp. 151-179.

Boxenbaum, E. (2006). Corporate Social Responsibility as Institutional Hybrids. *Journal of Business Strategies*, Vol. 23, No. 1, pp. 45-64.

Blumentritt, T. and Nigh, D. (2002). The Integration of Subsidiary Political Activities in Multinational Corporations. *Journal of International Business Studies*, Vol. 33, No. 1, pp. 57-77.

Chandler, A. D. and Mazlish, B. (Eds.) (2005). *Leviathans. Multinational Corporations and the New Global History*. Cambridge, UK: Cambridge University Press.

Christmann, P. (2004). Multinational Corporations and the Natural Environment: Determinants of Corporate Environmental Policy Standardization. *Academy of Management Journal*, Vol. 47, No. 5, pp. 747-760.

Cruz, L. B. and Boehe, D. M. (2010). How do Leading Retail MNCs Leverage CSR Globally? Insights from Brazil. *Journal of Business Ethics*, Vol. 91, pp. 243-263.

Donaldson, J. (2001). Multinational Enterprises, Employment Relations and Ethics. *Employee Relations*, Vol. 23, No. 6, pp. 627-642.

Eweje, G. (2006). The Role of MNEs in Community Development Initiatives in Developing Countries. *Business and Society*, Vol. 45, No. 2, pp. 93-129.

Hillman, A. J. and Wan, W. P. (2005). The Determinants of MNE Subsidiaries' Political Strategies: Evidence of Institutional Duality. *Journal of International Business Studies*, Vol. 36, pp. 322-340.

Husted, B. and Allen, D. (2006). Corporate Social Responsibility in the Multinational Enterprise: Strategic and Institutional Approaches. *Journal of International Business Studies*, Vol. 37, pp. 838-849.

Ite, U. E. (2004). Multinationals and Corporate Social Responsibility in developing Countries: A Case Study of Shell in Nigeria. *Corporate Social Responsibility and Environmental Management*, Vol. 11, No. 1, pp. 1-11.

Ite, U. E. (2005). Poverty Reduction in Resource-Rich Developing Countries: What Have Multinational Corporations Got To Do With It?. *Journal of International Development*, Vol. 17, No. 7, pp. 913-929.

Jamali, D. (2010). The CSR of MNC Subsidiaries in Developing Countries: Global, Local, Substantive or Diluted?. *Journal of Business Ethics*, Vol. 93, pp. 181-200.

Jamali, D. (2010b). MNCs and international accountability standards through an institutional lens: Evidence of symbolic conformity or decoupling. *Journal of Business Ethics*, Vol. 95, No. 4, pp. 617-640.

Jamali, D. and Mirshak, R. (2010). Business-Conflict Linkages: Revisiting MNCs, CSR, and Conflict. *Journal of Business Ethics*, Vol. 93, pp. 443-464.

Jamali, D. and Neville, B. (2011). Convergence versus Divergence of CSR in Developing Countries: An Embedded Multi-Layered Institutional Lens. *Journal of Business Ethics*, Vol. 102, pp. 599-621.

Jenkins, R. (2005). Globalization, Corporate Social Responsibility and Poverty. *International Affairs*, Vol. 81, No. 3, pp. 525-540.

Jones, P., Comfort, D. and Hillier, D. (2005). Corporate Social Responsibility and the UK's Top Ten Retailers. *International Journal of Retail and Distribution Management*, Vol. 33, No. 12, pp. 882-892.

Khavul, S. and Bruton, G. D. (2013). Harnessing Innovation for Change: Sustainability and Poverty in Developing Countries. *Journal of Management Studies*, Vol. 50, No. 2, pp. 285-306.

Kolk, A. and Van Tulder, R. (2006). Poverty Alleviation as Business Strategy? Evaluating Commitments of Frontrunner Multinational Corporations. *World Development*, Vol. 24, No. 5, pp. 789-801.

Kolk, A. and Lenfant, F. (2010). MNC Reporting on CSR and Conflict in Central Africa. *Journal of Business Ethics*, Vol. 93, pp. 241-255.

Korten, D. (2001). *When Corporations Rule the World*. San Francisco: Berret-Koehler.

Kostova, T. and Roth, K. (2002). Adoption of an Organizational Practice by Subsidiaries of Multinational Corporations: Institutional and Relational Effects. *Academy of Management Journal*, Vol. 45, pp. 215-33.

Kostova, T. and Zaheer, S. (1999). Organizational Legitimacy under Conditions of Complexity: The Case of the Multinational Enterprise. *Academy of Management Review*, Vol. 24, No.1, pp. 64-81.

Logsdon, J. M. and Wood, D. J. (2005). Global Business Citizenship and Voluntary Codes of Ethical Conduct. *Journal of Business Ethics*, Vol. 59, pp. 55-67.

Matten, D. and Crane, A. (2005). Corporate Citizenship: Toward an Extended Theoretical Conceptualization. *Academy of Management Review*, Vol. 30, No. 1, pp. 166-179.

Matten, D. and Moon, J. (2008). Implicit and Explicit CSR: A Conceptual Framework for a Comparative Understanding of Corporate Social Responsibility. *The Academy of Management Review*, Vol. 33, No. 2, pp. 404-424.

Mohan, A. (2006). Global Corporate Social Responsibilities Management in MNCs. *Journal of Business Strategies*, Vol. 23, No. 1, pp. 9-32.

Muller, A. (2006). Global versus Local CSR strategies. *European Management Journal*, Vol. 24, No. 2-3, pp. 189-198.

Newenham-Kahindi, A. M. (2011). A Global Mining Corporation and Local Communities in the Lake Victoria Zone: The Case of Barrick Gold Multinational in Tanzania. *Journal of Business Ethics*, Vol. 99, pp. 253-282.

Rosenzweig, P. and Singh, J. (1991). Organizational Environments and the Multinational Enterprise. *Academy of Management Review*, Vol. 16, No. 2, pp. 340-361.

Scherer, A. and Palazzo, M. (2008). Globalization and Corporate Social Responsibility. In: *The Oxford Handbook of Corporate Social Responsibility* (Crane, A., McWilliams, A., Matten, D., Moon, J., and Siegel, D. Eds.), Oxford University Press, pp. 413-431.

Strike, V. M., Gao, J. and Bansal, P. (2006). Being Good While Being Bad: Social Responsibility and the Diversification of US Firms. *Journal of International Business Studies*, Vol. 37, pp. 850-862.

Suchman, M. C. (1995). Managing Legitimacy: Strategic and Institutional Approaches. *Academy of Management Review*, Vol. 20, No. 3, pp. 571-611.

Willke, H. and Willke, G. (2008). The Corporation as a Political Actor? A Systems Theory Perspective. In: *Handbook of Research on Global Citizenship* (Scherer, A. and Palazzo, G., Eds.), Edward Elgar, Cheltenham, UK, pp. 552-574.

Yang, X. and Rivers, C. (2009). Antecedents of CSR Practices in MNCs' Subsidiaries: A Stakeholder and Institutional Perspective. *Journal of Business Ethics*, Vol. 86, pp. 155-169.

In: Multinational's CSR Practices …   ISBN: 978-1-63463-479-3
Editor: Alidou Ouedraogo   © 2015 Nova Science Publishers, Inc.

Chapter 6

CORPORATE CHARITY AND PROFITABILITY

D. Crowther[1] and S. Seifi[2]
[1]De Montfort University, United Kingdom
[2]University Putra Malaysia, Malaysia

INTRODUCTION

Increasingly throughout the world there is developing a closer link between business and charities. In some respect this is being caused by the retreat of the state and reduced intervention in such matters as can be left to charitable organisations. In other respects businesses recognise their role in society and feel obligated to help others through charitable links. This has been a feature of business since the beginnings of economic activity but is changing in the present time.

Clearly there is benefit for charities in having a relationship with business but for a successful outcome there should also be a benefit for the business also. It is clear that there is such a benefit to business and the business is more profitable because of this relationship. But for this to be true there are certain conditions which must be fulfilled and we will examine these. We start by identifying three different types of relationship which might exist:

- Charitable giving
- Cause related marketing
- Employee volunteering

But first we will consider the relationship between ethical behaviour and profitability.

DOES ETHICAL BEHAVIOUR LEAD TO PROFIT?

It can be argued that social responsibility by an organisation is ensuring stakeholder welfare, and respecting the society as a whole. Making a profit in order to survive and prosper should not be frowned upon. However, some ethical organisations such as The Body Shop International plc emphasise that profit is made with a wider social responsibility, referred to as 'profit with principles'. Others such as the Co-operative Bank of the UK have turned ethics into a competitive advantage. It could be envisaged that part of such responsibility would be caring for the environment, a constituent part of the society within which the organisation operates. At its narrowest the triple bottom line is used as a framework for measuring and reporting corporate performance against economic, social and environmental parameters. At its broadest the term is used to capture the whole set of values, issues and processes that organisations must consider so as to minimise any possible harm resulting from their operations and activities. The term also refers to creating economic, social and environmental values. This would require clarity of organisational aims and objectives and consideration of all the stakeholders.

The three bottom lines, which are in a constant state of flux, due to social, economic and environmental pressures and conflicts represent society, the economy and the environment. Society depends on the economy and the economy is dependent on the global ecosystem, whose well being represents the ultimate bottom line. The creation of a positive and environmentally concerned and even committed corporate image could also lead to profits. This can be substantiated by an example from the US where it is estimated that more than $2000 billion (£1300 billion) of mutual fund and pension money has been redirected into organisations that are deemed socially responsible.

Based on utilitarianism[50] a rationally operated organisation would attempt to maximise its good and minimise its bad to ensure that there is a profit having balanced out the costs and income. Organisations have been traditionally interested in the bottom line where profit or loss is highlighted. This cost benefit analysis (CBA) can be regarded as a form of utility calculation. Businesses use utility curves to illustrate the outcome of their

---

[50] The philosophy which underpins all economic activity

various activities selecting those that yield the maximum in terms of achievement. Such an approach can also be applied to ethical and / or green issues. When an organisation uses a utility calculation or CBA, it compares and contrasts the good and the bad consequences of carrying out a certain act or operation, usually in monetary terms. However, a utilitarian / ethical analysis considers the good and bad results of such an act or operation on everyone affected by it.

A criticism of CBA is that not all costs and benefits have an easily calculable monetary value. For instance, there is no market to assess the value of fresh air or peace and quiet. Furthermore, the market value of some goods may be distorted due to a number of factors, making their true value difficult to calculate. From an economist's viewpoint the market value of goods does not always reflect their opportunity cost, as determined by the consumers' marginal rates of substitution: seen by economists as the proper measure of value. Some CBA, for example, involves calculating the value of a human life. Such calculations are needed for certain activities, not necessarily how much a human life is worth, but to enable organisations and individuals to compare alternatives where life may be in danger.

The advocates of CBA argue that it is a 'value laden' theory with at least the advantage that it is capable of making explicit value commitments, in order for them to be 'flagged' and properly taken into consideration. However, the validity of any CBA is largely dependent on the objectivity of those who carry it out. Its role in public decision making should not be neglected. Although efficiency in resource allocation does have benefits, it is not the society's only value and so this should not be the only means of making choices as a society. Economic gains can offer an important inducement for organisations to pursue such policies. In addition, there may also be by-products in the form of improved corporate image and enhanced reputation, both of which could contribute to competitive advantage. Furthermore, green marketing policies may require investing in more advanced technology or obtaining access to it, thus gaining competitive advantage. This again underpins the indivisibility and inter-relatedness of green marketing drivers. Thus organisations such as the Bodyshop and the Co-operative Bank have benefited financially (and otherwise) from their ethical approaches in the market place by so doing.

One way for organisations to substantiate their green credentials is to adopt the CERES Principles (Coalition of Environmentally Responsible Economies). The Valdez Principles established in the aftermath of the Exxon Valdez super tanker disaster were a precursor to CERES. The Socially Responsible Investing (SRI) movement created these Principles. The main philosophy behind the Principles is to make multinational corporations accountable for their corporate operations. Accountability (by corporations) is stressed as a basis for these principles. When applying the Principles to a supermarket chain, for instance, the following principles would be observed:

- Protection of the Biosphere
- Sustainable use of natural Resources
- Reduction and Disposal of Wastes
- Energy Conservation
- Risk Reduction
- Safer Products and Services
- Environmental Restoration
- Informing the Public (of possible dangers to health, safety and the environment, etc.)
- Management Commitment

Amongst the signatories are General Motors and Polaroid who would have implemented companywide environmental management. This has been reflected further in their overall marketing. A less stringent version of the CERES Principles, i.e. the Business Charter for Sustainable Development (BCSD) exists, and hundreds of organisations have subscribed to it. BCSD is the most widely adopted of green accounting pledges. BCSD's emphasis ranges from full cost accounting (of environmental impact) to sustainable management (Wasik, 1996).

The UK company, Combined Landfill Projects provided power for thousands of homes by using gas which would otherwise pollute the atmosphere (Fitzherbert, 1999). The company is treated with a great deal of respect by the present government as it would contribute towards its drive to generate 10% of the UK's electricity from renewable energy by the year 2010.

The oil companies' fairly recent environmental policies, such as BP and its recent press commercials (in the UK) aimed at portraying the organisation as a green company support the notion that being green is good for business. Furthermore, companies are becoming increasingly aware that it is not simply what they sell that matters but also what they stand for that is important. Investment in renewable energy initiatives by the oil companies can be seen as a proactive step to ensure future survival. During the period 1990-1997 while the sales of coal and oil grew by just over 1% per annum, geothermal power saw an increase of 3% whereas solar photovoltaic went up by 16.8% and wind power grew by a dramatic 25.7% (Brown et al., 1998).

The opportunity and the challenges are there for businesses to take advantage of, and a number of pro-active companies are doing so. The 980 million or so compact fluorescent light bulbs used today reduce electricity needs by the output of approximately 100 coal-fired power stations. When there are undeniable signs that consumers demand green and environmentally friendly products, proactive businesses can satisfy such needs at a profit.

A research carried out for the Institute of Business Ethics (IBE), found that companies that take ethical issues seriously, are generally better managed and more sustainable than those who do not. Those organisations that do not practice ethics because it is "right" may change their minds if they think it will make them more profitable.

SOCIAL VALUES

The idea that an organisation is not formed merely to provide benefit to its shareholders is not a new concept. Some owners of businesses have always recognised a responsibility to other stakeholders and this is evident from the early days of the Industrial Revolution. Thus, for example, Robert Owen (1816, 1991) demonstrated dissatisfaction with the assumption that only the internal effects of actions need be recorded through accounting. Furthermore he put his beliefs into practice through the inclusion within his sphere of industrial operations the provision of housing for his workers at New Lanark. Others went further still and Jedediah Strutt and his sons of Belpher[51], for example, provided farms to ensure that their workers received an adequate supply of milk, as well as building accommodation for their workforce which was of such high standard that these dwellings remain highly desirable in the present[52]. Similarly the Gregs of Quarry Bank provided education as well as housing for their workforce. Indeed Salt went further and attempted to provide a complete ecosphere for his workers[53]. Thus there is evidence from

---

[51] A small town in the centre of England

[52] Indeed the earlier workers' accommodation provided by Richard Arkwright, arguably the instigator of the Industrial Revolution, at Cromford, Derbyshire, remain equally desirable.

[53] The illustrations cited hear are all from various parts of the UK and all from the late 18th and early 19th centuries. This is not just because one of the authors is English but also because the Industrial Revolution commenced in the UK.

throughout the history of modernity[54] that the self-centred approach of concern only with the organisation and its owners was not universally acceptable and was unable to satisfactorily provide a basis for human activity.

Many organisations have always recognised that they exist within society and must at least partly meet the needs of all of that society. Attempting this task of meeting differing requirements is based upon a recognition of their own position in the community and the values upon which they are founded. This was recognised by Selznick (1957: 136) who stated:

> "Truly accepted values must infuse the organisation at many levels, affecting the perspective and attitudes of personnel, the relative importance of staff activities, the distribution of authority, relations with outside groups, and many other matters. Thus if a large corporation asserts the wish to change its role in the community from a narrow emphasis on profit-making to a large social responsibility (even though the ultimate goal remains some combination of survival and profit-making ability), it must explore the implications of such a change for decision making in a wide variety of organisational activities."

The ethical implications of a firm's behaviour were considered by McCoy (1985: 87) who considers ethics to be at the core of business behaviour. He states:

> "Dealing with values required continual monitoring of the surrounding environment, weighing alternative courses of action, balancing and (when possible) integrating conflicting responsibilities, setting priorities among competing goals, and establishing criteria for defining and evaluating performance. Along with these goes learning ways to bring this ethical reflection directly and fully into the processes by which policy is made, implemented, and evaluated. Increasingly, skills in dealing with values as integral components of performance and policy-making are being recognised as central for effective management in a society and a world undergoing rapid change."

The way in which a business performs in terms of its ethical behaviour and identified place in society as a whole is determined by its relationship with its stakeholder community. It is also to some extent determined by, as well as to some extent determining, the culture of the organisation. Kotter and Heskett

---

[54] Examples from pre-modernity also exist primarily in the form of assistance provided by religious institutions to anyone in need. The essential point is that socially responsible behaviour has always existed from people / organisations who care and has been unrelated to any form of regulation.

(1992) consider corporate culture and show how this can lead to good business performance but also to bad business performance and a lack of ability to change to match changing environmental conditions. They consider that effective leadership is crucial to success. Success, like good performance, is always of course a subjective construct depending upon the perspective of the evaluator. When we consider NGOs of course that success becomes even more subjective as there are no yardsticks such as profit; consequently different metrics are needs, including qualitative metrics and it would be useful to research what is needed and what is used.

CHARITABLE DONATIONS

The idea that an organisation is not formed merely to provide benefit to its shareholders is not a new concept. Some owners of businesses have always recognised a responsibility to other stakeholders and this is evident from the early days of the industrial Revolution. This is still apparent and many organisations give to charity without even mentioning that they are doing so. Indeed in the UK this is very prevalent, as it is across much of Europe. This is particularly common for smaller organisations which tend to be focused on their local community and regularly donate. For local community focused businesses this tends to be known about and therefore has benefits to the business in terms of increased sales. For larger businesses it tends to be anonymous and therefore gives no benefit to that business.

It is however generally necessary to account for the activities of an organisation in terms of its social performance. A model for the analysis of social performance can be illustrated as:

Statement of Social Income:	£
Value generated by the productive process	xxx
+ unappropriable benefits	xxx
- external costs imposed on the community	xxx
Net social value created	xxx

Social marketing predominantly focuses upon social and health issues, concentrating on the activities of not for profit organisations such as ASH

(Action on Smoking and Health) and INWAT (International Network of Women Against Tobacco). However recently commercial organisations such as Nike and Daewoo, have also begun to embrace such concepts. Such activity has been described as the new philanthropic paradigm. It is suggested that one way of commercial organisations applying marketing principles to social and health issues is through the cultivation of social alliances typically with non commercial organisations. An illustration of such is Nike's alliance with Imperial Cancer in arranging organised runs around the London area, encouraging individuals to keep active and healthy. Such initiatives have the potential to benefit society through an increased number of healthier individuals and hence less potential burden on the health services, whilst at the same time, helping to reinforce the Nike brand and therefore help to advance its business goals.

It has been suggested that such alliances are evidence of broader changes happening in society, specifically that the government considers its responsibilities towards society's problems as both diminishing and changing. Further to this they suggest that given the cut backs in government spending and increased competitiveness amongst non profit making organisations for existing funds, there is every likelihood that social alliances will increase in popularity. Social marketing can be differentiated from commercial marketing by its characteristics:

Social Marketing	Commercial Marketing
Wants to do good	Wants to make money
Funded by taxes, donations	Funded by investments and loans
Publicly accountable	Privately accountable
Performance hard to measure by normal means	Performance measured in profits, market share
Behavioural goals long term	Behavioural goals short term
Often target controversial behaviours	Provides non-controversial products/services
Often choose high-risk targets	Choose accessible targets
Risk averse managers	Risk taking managers
Participative decision-making	Hierarchical decision-making
Relationships based upon trust	Relationships often competitive

CAUSE RELATED MARKETING

Many businesses are attempting to align their social responsibility agendas with their business motivations. This trend has been driven by the society's heightened expectations and increased criticism by several interest groups such as environmental activists, human rights groups, and consumer associations.

The effort is placed on 'marrying' the corporate strategy of community involvement with social issues related to their business. Cause Related Marketing (CRM) is a prime example of the partnership formed between corporations and charities to raise both money and brand awareness and demonstrate a corporation's socially responsible behaviour.

CRM can be used by businesses to achieve their marketing objectives whilst addressing the long-term interests of the society. Today businesses operate in a highly competitive and hostile environment dominated by many gatekeeper groups which can hinder their efforts in gaining access to markets or achieving their marketing objectives. Consumer associations, trade unions, environmental groups, human rights groups, local communities, government agencies and the media act as gatekeepers due to their power and role as watchdogs for the many groups of people whose interests they promote and protect.

If a business can actively demonstrate that it acknowledges the concerns and even criticisms raised by these stakeholder groups by for example adapting its business practices and launching community involvement programmes, it can enhance its corporate reputation, the picture that different stakeholder groups have about the organisation.

CRM focuses on partnerships/relationships between businesses and non-profit organizations, charities, and charitable causes. These partnerships have the potential to instill trust, develop positive attitudes and perceptions towards the business and subsequently strengthen the corporate image.

Some of the key success factors to a cause related marketing project are:

- Evaluate your organization's values and current image: Where do you stand in the minds of your target? Do you want to be seen as young, contemporary or responsible? How visible are you?
- Lay down the objectives clearly: After you have reached a consensus on your objective, try to map it with a cause or charity mission that has a synergy. You will need the co-operation of your colleagues. Associate with a cause that can be understood and felt by your target.

- Is the relationship short or long term? You will have to decide that. Where do you want to be perceived in your domain matrix? What are the time implications - is it short or long term?
- Get your organization geared for the challenge in the relationship: Ensure top management approval and employee participation. Drill down deeper into the heart of the tie up.
- Visualize the results ahead of time: Is it going to be a surge in sales, or a high recall among your target. Or your organization being perceived as a socially responsible body, which goes beyond the duty of business. Or to simply add to the brand image. To improve the quality and extent of contribution.
- Consumers want socially responsible organizations: Research show that consumers actively want corporates to advertise their charitable actions, show tangible results and have long duration of these missions. There is a great likelihood that consumers will switch brands if they find that an organization is associated with a good cause, while other factors remain equal.
- Positive image makes a difference: A high percentage of consumers researched claim to have a positive image of a company which they see making the world a better place or have charity initiatives as part of their business policy. (Source: The Winning Game: Business in the Community/Research International 1996).
- Build a human face to the whole event: Being visual is effective. Have a theme, relate it to the target, build an icon or a mnemonic and carry it through all forms of communication.
- Reliability is key: Tie up with a reliable, leading honest charity mission. Nothing can be more distressing than a mission gone awry due to unreliable partners.
- Face to face is the best approach: Try to make the program one on one. Making a program interactive takes it that extra mile.
- Have idea, will travel: Have a campaignable idea. An idea that can be run across media and without any hiccups.
- A significant ad and communication budget is required: Depending on the budget, involve celebrities to help generate funds. A significant ad and communication budget is required. There are of course relationships that are done on shoestring budgets also, like the BMW tie up with the Susan B Comen Breast Cancer Foundation, which

worked on a commitment from test-drives for women across the US, while lionizing local heroes and doctors.

- Monitor the results closely: Are you getting the mileage you expected? Are both parties reaping the fruits of labor? Is the review plan in place?

Trust is the relationship but keep a contingency plan in place: Has the brand or corporate being adequately protected? Is the partnership prudent? Is there a clear exit strategy, terms, and clauses?

EMPLOYEE VOLUNTEERING

Employee volunteering (EV), has been described as the fastest growing form of corporate community support and indeed one of the core components of CSR. In the endless quest for a competitive advantage, corporations are increasingly recognizing the value of CSR and EV. It has been suggested that EV is emerging as one of the most cost-effective methods to show community commitment whilst gaining rich and multiple rewards that have a direct impact in the business bottom line. Corporations have many options to choose from in order to demonstrate their CSR behaviour: sponsorships, financial contribution, gifts in kind, partnerships, cause-related-marketing, and employee volunteering. The growth in EV is part of the wider movement to encourage the corporate sector to 'tangibly' demonstrate commitment to enhancing the well-being of the society and accountability for its actions.

Employee volunteering is one way in which corporations can fulfill expectations and moral obligations at the level of society and hence, demonstrate that they are socially responsible. When businesses engage in corporate volunteering they actively support and encourage their employees to volunteer their services to a local charitable organization. It is an initiative in which the corporation supports and encourages employees, retail partners, and/or franchise members to *volunteer* their time to support local community organizations and causes."

Volunteer efforts may encompass of the following: expertise, talents, ideas, and/or physical labour whereas, corporate support may involve recognition for volunteer service, provision of paid time off from work, match services to help employees find opportunities of interest, formation of teams to support specific causes.

"Corporate volunteering is any formal or organized means a company uses to encourage and support its employees and retirees (and possibly their families) to volunteer their time and skills in the service of the community." (The Association of Volunteer Services, 2006).

It might include the following:

- Provision of information and encouragement of employees to volunteer on their own time
- Provision of rewards and incentives to employees who volunteer
- Encouragement of employees to work for a one-time project or an ongoing program established by a non-profit organization
- Plan a volunteer project for a company to serve the community

What is the attraction in adopting EV? The National Centre for Volunteering in the UK claims that everyone involved benefits – the corporation that provides volunteers, the organizations where employee volunteers help out, the wider community, and the employees themselves. There is worldwide evidence that illustrates that EV is on the rise. The 1997 National Survey of Volunteering found that in the UK a significant number of people (around 22 million or 48% of the population) were involved in volunteering projects in the previous year (Smith 1998). A 1998 Charities Aid Foundation study, indicated that one in three large UK businesses have formal EV programmes. In their report, the International Conference Volunteers, a Geneva-based NGO that connects potential volunteers to organizers of non-profit projects, state that many European countries have witnessed an increase in the last five years in the number of businesses, public and voluntary sector organizations that are involved in EV.

There is ample evidence of the benefits derived by all parties from EV. This justifies the growth and popularity of the concept in the business sector. Benefits can be described as follows:

Benefits for the employer
- Exhibits commitment to building healthy communities
- Develops skills and enhances morale among the workforce
- Enhances corporate image
- Reinforces organisational loyalty

Benefits for the employee
- Offers the satisfaction of contributing to society
- Develops new skills and improves existing ones
- Offers a break from the daily work routine
- Increases motivation

Benefits for the volunteer-involving organization and the community
- Builds up the supply of volunteers
- Enhances the skills and competencies of volunteers
- Creates partnerships with the corporate and the public sectors
- Contributes to breaking down barriers between different sections of society

SOCIAL IMPACT ASSESSMENT

Social impact assessment is not new; actually it has been around in the not for profit sector for about 40 years. At that time (the early 1970s) CBA – as costs benefit analysis was known – was considered to be the latest technique to evaluate the non-financial aspects of a projects impact. Given that it was used primarily by such organisations as local authorities then, the non-financial impact was of course primarily social impact. From this it was expected at the time that CBA would become a widespread tool for analysis but this never really happened and the prime reason why it never happened was the almost total absence of suitable metrics to incorporate into the analysis, meaning that the evaluation was primarily base upon judgement of nice phrases. And consequently the technique was never really adopted outside of the public sector and never became a serious tool to help commercial managers in their decision making.

Times have changed over the last 40 years and now there is a growing concern and recognition that the activities of an organisation impact upon the external environment. Thus such activity has become of increasing concern to the stakeholders of the organisation who have become increasingly voluble in expressing their expectations. Indeed these other stakeholders have not just an interest in the activities of the organisation but also a degree of influence over the shaping of those activities. This influence is so significant that it can be argued that the power and influence of these stakeholders is such that it amounts to quasi-ownership of the organisation. Central to this is a concern for the future which has become manifest through the term sustainability. This term sustainability has become ubiquitous both within the discourse on globalisation and within the discourse on corporate performance. Sustainability is of course a controversial issue and there are many definitions of what is meant by the term. At the broadest level any definition of sustainability is concerned with the effect which action taken in the present has upon the options available in the future. If resources are utilised in the present then they are no longer available for use in the future, and this is of particular concern if the resources are finite in quantity. Thus raw materials of an extractive nature, such as coal, iron or oil, are finite in quantity and once used are not available for future use. At some point in the future therefore alternatives will be needed to fulfil the functions currently provided by these resources. This may be at some point in the relatively distant future but of more immediate concern is the fact that as resources become depleted then the cost of acquiring the remaining resources tends to increase, and hence the operational costs of organisations tend to increase.[55] Sustainability therefore implies that society must use no more of a resource than can be regenerated. This can be defined in terms of the carrying capacity of the ecosystem and described with input–output models of resource consumption. So metrics are starting to appear which help measure the impact of organisational activity.

The real reason for undertaking a social impact assessment (SIA) is to measure the degree to which project funders, sponsors and stakeholders will receive the outcomes from the project that they seek. SIA is thus not a technical exercise by which the 'experts' talk to each other about what might – or should – happen. It is a process by which the project initiators use experts to help them conduct a dialogue about outcomes and expectations; measuring the impact that will be created along the dimensions of the project where they seek change.

There are various methodologies by which this assessment can be performed.

CONSIDERING ACTUAL PRACTICE

It is fairly general that companies recognise the benefits which accrue from connections with NGOs and various charitable activities. This is true

---

[55] Similarly once an animal or plant species becomes extinct then the benefits of that species to the environment can no longer be accrued. In view of the fact that many pharmaceuticals are currently being developed from plant species still being discovered, this may be significant for the future.

worldwide and examples abound of such practice as companies have realised the benefits of such arrangements. For example Sime Darby is a Malaysian conglomerate company with operations throughout the Far East. In addition to its operations it has an extensive range of associations with local charities and NOGs extending throughout Malaysia and also in China, Malaysia, Indonesia and Vietnam. These activities include health awareness, poverty alleviation and sports facilities as well as environmental protection and charitable donations. Thus Sime Darby Plantation has embarked on a forest tree planting programme in its estates since 2008. The trees include indigenous, endangered and rare species of tropical forest trees. The aim is to establish a gene pool of these species apart from enriching the biodiversity estates. As at November 2011, a total of 329,225 trees from 276 species have been planted within Sime Darby Plantation's Malaysian estates. These numbers include some 10,450 forest trees which have been planted at Wildlife Sanctuary on Carey Island since 2008. The management has allocated close to 100 hectares in Carey Island's West Estate for this project to enrich the biodiversity of the island.

The Stability of Altered Forest Environment (SAFE) Project is a long-term research project which is a collaboration between YSD (Yayasan Sime Darby) and South East Asia Rainforest Research Programme (SEARRP)- an overseas research programme of the Royal Society (The UK and Commonwealth Academy of Science). SAFE is slated to be the world's largest ecological experiment both in terms of size and breadth of ecological processes. The project will allow insights to minimise biodiversity impacts while maximising ecosystem services. The fully integrated research programme will focus on these key areas: animal and plant diversity, water and soils, carbon cycling, nutrient cycling and microclimate. The central element is the creation of clusters of forest patches on an hectare, 10 hectares and 100 hectares within an oil palm plantation which is being established by Yayasan Sabah. The research plots are to be established in the surrounding (new) oil palm plantations, in mature plantations, areas of logged forests on land belonging to Yayasan Sabah, and in undisturbed primary forests in the Maliau Basin. Sime Darby Plantation signed a Memorandum of Understanding with the Sabah Forestry Department on January 29, 2008 pledging RM25 million towards the conservation of 5,403 hectares of the Ulu Segama Forest Reserve – home to 5,000 Orangutans. The Ulu Segama Forest Reserve covers 250,000 hectares of which 160,000 hectares have been overlogged and in need of restoration and rehabilitation.

The Bornean Sumatran Rhino is considered a critically endangered species, with only 50 individuals existing in the wild, and about 30 may be found in Sabah. The Borneo Rhinoceros Sanctuary (BRS) provides a natural environment suitable for the rhinos offering protection from poachers and hunters and have their well-being monitored by qualified staff. It is hoped that once brought into this sanctuary, the rhinos will mate and breed, thus boosting the dangerously low numbers of the species and ensuring its survival. YSD has allocated RM5 million towards this cause from 2009 to 2012. The BRS is an initiative by the Borneo Rhinoceros Alliance (BORA) and involves the creation and maintenance of a fenced-off area within the Tabin Wildlife Reserve. At present, there is a male and an aged female rhino in the sanctuary, and hopefully another young female sighted in the wild in Tabin may be rescued and relocated to the sanctuary for breeding. In November 2010, Yayasan Sime Darby, Sime Darby Plantation and WWF-Malaysia signed an agreement to carry out a study on selected estates to formulate recommendations to improve sustainable plantation management. The Sime Darby Plantation estate chosen was the Sungai Dingin Estate in Kedah. In a study conducted by the Sabah Wildlife Department (SWD) in 2005, it was found that the population size of the Proboscis monkey was estimated to be a minimum of 5,907 individuals along major coastal river systems in Sabah. However, only 15.3% of the estimated population were found within protected forest reserves, with much of the species diminishing habitat exposed to further conversion, extraction and disturbance. This has led to increased isolation of proboscis monkey groups. YSD's contribution towards the conservation and management of the Proboscis monkey in Sabah is via efforts to build capacity in the area of conservation biology and wildlife management within the SWD. This is done through the higher education training (PhD) of a senior wildlife officer, Dr Senthilvel Nathan at Cardiff University, and Masters degree courses of two other staff. This programme also works towards the rescue and translocation operations of pocketed populations of Proboscis monkeys in adverse habitats.

Similarly Petronas is the national oil company of Malaysia, given the entire ownership and control of the petroleum resources in the country. In the last 40 years it has since grown from merely being the manager and regulator of Malaysia's upstream sector into a fully integrated oil and gas corporation, ranked among the FORTUNE Global 500® largest corporations in the world. Alongside these operations it also engages with charitable and socially responsible activities. Thus the Petronas Volunteer Opportunity Programme collaborates with selected NGOs and relevant parties to scout for volunteer opportunities and provide necessary training, direction and support to develop skills useful in programmes such as disaster rehabilitation and education outreach activities. Petronas has also embraced its role as a leading patron of the arts in Malaysia to support, create and promote accessible platforms for the visual arts, performing arts and classical music in new ways for society to appreciate rich and relevant cultural experiences. Going beyond the conventional corporate sponsorship of activities in the area of arts and culture, they have established an art gallery, a concert hall, a philharmonic orchestra and a performing arts group to provide an avenue for the public to experience world-class arts and cultural activities as well as to appreciate Malaysia's traditional heritage afresh.

A similar range of activities can be found at all large companies throughout Asia as well as throughout the western world.

CONCLUSION

There are various aspects to the relationship between businesses and charities but increasingly they are all seen as beneficial to both parties. And for business this effectively means increased profitability. This profitability is manifest in the short term through increased sales and in the longer term through improved reputation being translated into increased sales and profitability. This is perfectly in accordance with the principles of corporate social responsibility which show that the best companies perform well financially while also performing well both socially and environmentally.

REFERENCES

Brown, L., Renner, M., & Flavin, C. (1998). *Vital signs The Environmental Trends that are Shaping our Future.* London: Earthscan.

FitzHerbert, D. (1999). Electricity generating renewables and global warming emissions. Renewable energy, Vol.16, No. 1, pp. 1057-1063.

Kotter, J.P., & Heskett J.L. (1992). Corporate Culture and Performance. New York, The Free Press.

McCoy, C.S. (1985). Management of Values: The Ethical Difference in Corporate Policy and Performance. Marshfield, Mass, Pitman.

Owen, R. (1991). A New View of Society and other writings, London, Penguin.

Selznick, N. (1957). Leadership in Administration: A Sociological Interpretation. Evanston, Ill; Row, Peterson.

Smith, D. (1998). The 1997 National Survey of Volunteering, Institute for Volunteering Research

Wasik, J.F. (1996). *Green Marketing and Management: a global perspective.* Blackwell

FURTHER READING

Crowther, D., & Aras, G. (2013). *The Governance of Risk.* Bingley; Emerald.

Ashley, P., & Crowther, D. (2012). *Territories of Social Responsibility: Opening the policy agenda.* Farnham; Gower.

Aras, G., & Crowther, D. (2012). *Business Strategy and Sustainability.* Bingley; Emerald.

Crowther, D., & Davila Gomez, A.M. (2012). *Human Dignity and Managerial Responsibility: diversity, rights and sustainability*; Farnham; Gower.

Aras, G., & Crowther, D. (2012). *Governance and Social Responsibility.* London; Macmillan.

Seifi, S., & Crowther, D. (2011). *Corporate Governance and International Business.* Copenhagen; Ventus.

Aras, G., & Crowther, D. (2011). *Governance in the Business Environment.* Bingley; Emerald.

Aras, G., & Crowther, D. (2010). *NGOs and Social Responsibility.* Bingley; Emerald.

Aras, G., & Crowther, D. (2010). *Gower Handbook of Corporate Governance and Social Responsibility.* Farnham; Gower.

Seifi, S., & Crowther, D. (2010). *Corporate Governance and Risk Management.* Copenhagen; Ventus.

Aras, G., & Crowther, D. (2009). *The Durable Corporation: strategies for sustainable development.* Farnham; Gower.

Aras, G. & Crowther, D. (2009). *Global Perspectives on Corporate Governance and Corporate Social Responsibility.* Farnham; Gower.

Aras, G., Crowther, D., & Vettori, S. (2009). *Corporate Social Responsibility in SMEs.* SRRNet, Leicester.

Aras, G., & Crowther, D. (2008). *Introduction to Corporate Social Responsibility.* Copenhagen; Ventus.

Crowther, D., & Caliyurt, K.T. (2008). *Globalisation and Social Responsibility.* 2nd Edition; Cambridge; Cambridge Scholars Press.

Crowther, D., & Capaldi, N. (2008). *Ashgate Research Companion to Corporate Social Responsibility*. Aldershot; Ashgate.

BIOGRAPHIES

David Crowther, PhD (www.davideacrowther.com) is Professor of Corporate Social Responsibility and Head of the Centre for Research into Organisational Governance at De Montfort University, Leicester, UK and Visiting Professor at various locations. He is a qualified accountant with many years' business experience. His research is into corporate social responsibility with a particular emphasis on the relationship between social, environmental and financial performance. David has published over 40 books and has also contributed more than 350 articles to academic, business and professional journals and to edited book collections. He has also spoken widely at conferences and seminars and acted as a consultant to a wide range of government, professional and commercial organisations. He is a member of a number of international advisory boards and is also founding Chair of the Social Responsibility Research Network; Series Editor of the Gower Applied Research in Corporate Social Responsibility book series and the Emerald Developments in Corporate Governance and Responsibility book series; Founding Editor of Social Responsibility Journal; and Convenor of the International Conference Series on Corporate Social Responsibility, now in its 13th year.

Shahla Seifi (www.shahlaseifi.com) was employed by ISIRI – the Institute of Standards and Industrial Research of Iran – and based in Tehran prior to her marriage to David. In this capacity she was a member of the Iranian Shadow ISO 26000 working group. Her main concerns are with aspects of sustainability and the development of appropriate consumer information to assist socially responsible choices. She is currently completing a PhD at Universiti Putra Malaysia while being based in the UK. She has been the secretary of many Iranian national standards (more than 200) and together with David, has recently authored two books on relevant topics; she has previously translated the 11 ISO development manuals for the developing countries which were the basis for teaching standardisation in Iran. She has also authored two other books the details of which can be found in her website.

In: Multinational's CSR Practices ...
Editor: Alidou Ouedraogo

ISBN: 978-1-63463-479-3
© 2015 Nova Science Publishers, Inc.

Chapter 7

LABOUR RIGHTS IN GLOBAL SUPPLY CHAINS: AN OXFAM CASE STUDY OF UNILEVER IN VIETNAM

R. Wilshaw and E. Sahan
Oxfam Great Britain

1. INTRODUCTION

Global supply chains can be powerful levers in the fight against poverty. They can bring in wealth and jobs, expertise and technology, and goods and services to regions and people around the world. Those that connect production facilities in the developing world to consumers in the developed world can be particularly important in helping generate economic growth, bringing trade and investment to poorer regions and people. However, the quality of this growth and whether it is able to tackle poverty hinges, at least partly, on whether the rights of the most vulnerable people are respected and they are empowered to enjoy them.

The biggest brands yield the most power. The sheer scale of their purchasing gives them enormous power over their suppliers[56]. How these global brands choose to use this power matters immensely for workers in their supply chain, particularly in developing countries.

---

[56] Oxfam (2010) 'Better Jobs in Better Supply Chains' an Oxfam briefing for business.

This chapter uses a case study to explore labor standards in the Viet Nam operations and supply chain of Unilever. Unilever is one of the largest companies in the world, with revenues of over $58 billion, a presence in over 100 countries and the majority of its business in developing countries. With over 160,000 suppliers around the world linking into its supply chains, the company has a tangible impact on hundreds of thousands of workers[57]. Most of the issues faced by Unilever in improving working conditions in its supply chain are common to its competitors, both food and beverage companies and home/personal care companies. For this reason, the Oxfam believes that the lessons from this case study are valid for a range of industry sectors and can be used to help improve conditions for workers in global supply chains around the world. Oxfam CEO Barbara Stocking welcomed Unilever's willingness to open its operations and supply chain to the scrutiny of its research team, as demonstrating an exceptional level of transparency and a genuine commitment to stakeholder engagement.

This article is based on the Executive Summary and Introduction sections of the report 'Labour rights in Unilever's supply chain: From compliance towards good practice; an Oxfam study of labour issues in Unilever's Viet Nam operations and supply chain', carried out with Unilever's co-operation and published by Oxfam in February 2013 (available in English and Vietnamese).

2. TACKLING LABOUR ISSUES IN GLOBAL SUPPLY CHAINS

Labor rights are about people and the quality of their productive working lives. The starting point for respecting human and labor rights is to understand the impact of a business's actions on people.

> "Labor rights should be at the heart of [a company's reporting framework] as there is nothing more material to the way a business runs than its labor. Workers build the wealth."

> Dan Rees, ILO Better Work program[58]

---

[57] R.Wilshaw with Liesbeth Unger, Do Quynh Chi and Pham Thu Thuy (2013) 'Labour rights in Unilever's supply chain: From compliance towards good practice'; an Oxfam study of labour issues in Unilever's Viet Nam operations and supply chain', Oxford: Oxfam.

[58] D. Rees (2011) Director - ILO Better Work program, in interview with Oxfam on 17 November 2011.

Companies often express disappointment when workers tell an undercover reporter about violations they have not communicated to a supervisor, auditor or helpline, fearing the consequences. A manager may say 'my door is always open to workers'. But this is not the same as measuring a manufacturing defect rate or the level of pollution in water; workers weigh up the consequences before voicing a concern.

For Oxfam, respect for labor rights and a guarantee of good-quality jobs are core elements of corporate responsibility and are key to ensuring international trade enables people to work their way out of poverty. Respect for human and labor rights is fundamental to a company's commitment to achieve the 'triple bottom line' of economic, environmental and social sustainability. Yet evidence suggests that global supply chains of all kinds are dogged by endemic problems, including weak relations between management and workers, poverty wages, exhausting working hours and precarious employment.

Since the sweatshop campaigns of the 1990s, companies have endeavored to ensure compliance with their codes of conduct through top-down methods such as making this a condition of contract and imposing audits and corrective actions on supplier sites.

Competing in business through containing wage costs is still the most common approach to wage policies. A survey of wage issues in factories in ten countries by the Fair Wage Network found that none of the 15 Vietnamese factories surveyed paid above the minimum wage and half underpaid those wages. The survey also highlighted the widespread use of double record-keeping at factories in order to 'pass' a social audit.

Imposing expectations of compliance on suppliers can drive secrecy about issues which have a high impact on workers. In Oxfam's experience, audits can be a helpful tool for identifying more visible issues in workplaces to which companies have a direct line of sight, but they are 'a weak tool for social upgrading', according to recent in-depth research.[59]No amount of audits and corrective actions will achieve compliance in a context of endemic non-compliance, and their limitations are ever more apparent: 'at best they are a health check, at worst they mask problems'.[60]

---

[59] Capturing the Gains for Workers and Suppliers in Global Value Chains is an international research network funded by DFID and involving researchers in 20 countries in Africa, Asia, Latin America and USA. For more information, visit: www.capturingthegains.org

[60] P. McAllister (2011) Director - Ethical Trading Initiative, ETI Members' Meeting March 2011.

"Over the last 15 years brands and purchasers tried valiantly to cajole, persuade, regulate and instruct their suppliers and sub-contractors to comply with local law and international standards on decent work. However none of these have made a noticeable dent in the systemic abuse of workers' rights in global supply chains."

R. Hurst (2011)[61]

Poor working conditions may be exacerbated by other issues that are not within the ability of a company to address. For example, governments may be unable or unwilling to ensure protection for workers and to apply the law fully, trade unions may be repressed, and the capacity of all parties to address the issues may be limited. One way to look at the key issues impacting workers is as a sequence of root causes which helps illustrate why achieving compliance on. The below diagram is an example of how we can understand the root causes of excessive working hours (one of the four issues explored in the study).

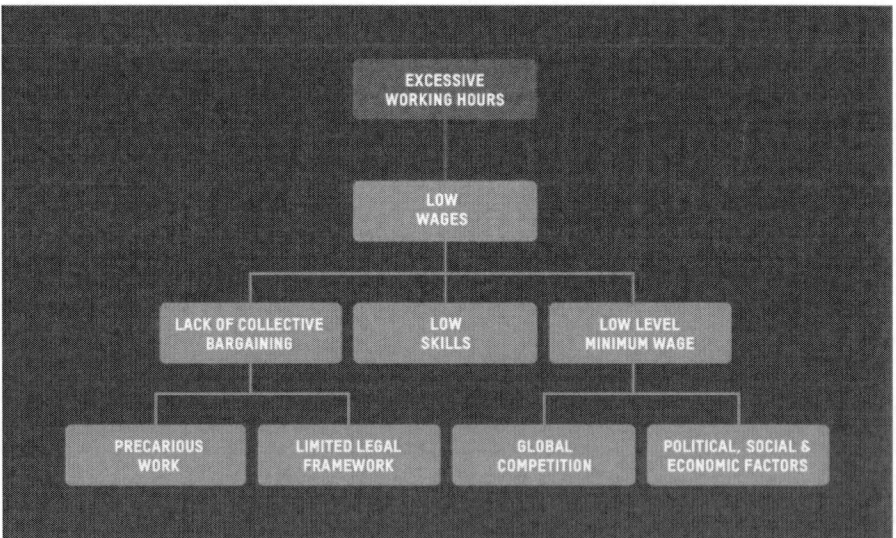

Sources: "Labor rights in Unilever's supply chain: From compliance towards good practice; an Oxfam study of labor issues in Unilever's Viet Nam operations and supply chain", Oxfam, 2013.

Figure 1. Root causes of excessive working hours.

---

[61] R. Hurst (2011) 'Finding the sweet spot: Smarter ethical trade that delivers more for all', London: Impactt, http://www.impacttlimited.com/resources/resources-part-1

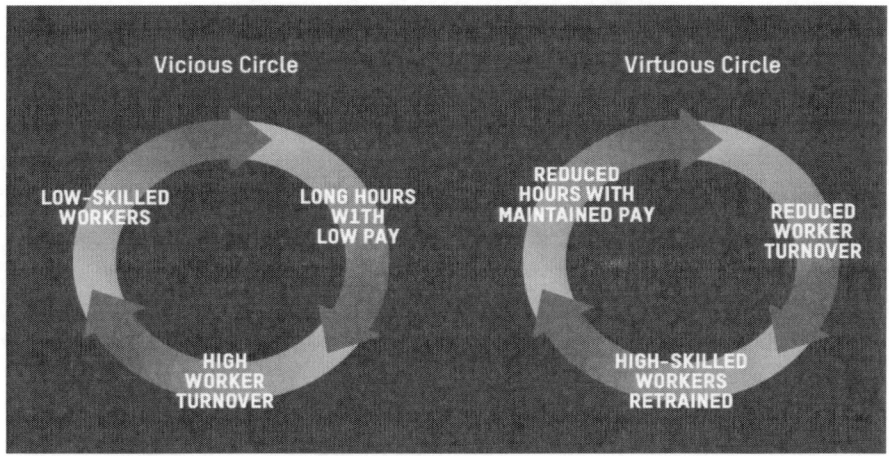

Sources: "Labor rights in Unilever's supply chain: From compliance towards good practice; an Oxfam study of labor issues in Unilever's Viet Nam operations and supply chain", Oxfam, 2013.

Figure 2. Achieving a virtuous circle in the workplace.

A multinational company operating in a variety of countries, with a supply chain comprising thousands of suppliers, needs proven, scalable solutions to these challenges. There is increasing interest in what it would take to achieve a virtuous circle in workplaces, in which greater respect for rights has a positive reinforcing effect on productivity, quality, worker satisfaction and retention.

To achieve sustainable solutions collaboration is needed with other companies, trade unions, NGOs and governments that share a good understanding of the issues concerned. They need to work together towards a culture of compliance with the rule of law and international labor standards, together with mature systems of industrial relations. Promoting ethical behavior may involve advocating for governments to fulfil their duties and help workers overcome obstacles to realize their rights.

3. BACKGROUND AND PURPOSE OF THE OXFAM UNILEVER STUDY

The study was initiated by Oxfam and Unilever, based on a long period of dialogue on sustainable agriculture within the Sustainable Food Lab, a multi-stakeholder initiative. The relationship developed following a ground-breaking poverty footprint study of Unilever's operations in Indonesia in 2005. In 2009, when reviewing the risks of a proposed new collaborative project on smallholder agriculture, one of the risks identified was Unilever's management of labour rights. The accompanying report is the result of subsequent dialogue on this issue. Funded by Oxfam, the study had two objectives:

Objective 1: To assess the labor standards in Unilever's operations and wider supply chain, taking into account international standards and local conditions.

Objective 2: To develop a set of principles and measures to guide Unilever, and other companies, in fulfilling their social responsibilities, as a complement to the better-defined environmental measures available.

Unilever stated that it would like to gain a better understanding of the issues that are important to workers but difficult for companies to measure and manage. The Fast Moving Consumer Goods sector is at an early stage of dealing with these kinds of issues. For instance, it is still developing an understanding of what is a Living Wage and the implications of adopting a Living Wage. To help Unilever and the broader industry develop a better understand of and approaches to dealing with key issues impacting workers, the study focused on four issues:

1. **Freedom of association and collective bargaining:** These were selected as they are enabling rights for the realization of decent working conditions[62]. They are among the fundamental rights of the International Labor Organization (ILO)[63]. The study looked at whether workers could exercise these rights despite the limitations imposed by Vietnamese law.

2. **Living Wage:** This concept is gaining increased attention and causing heated debate among companies, trade unions and non-government organizations (NGOs) across the world. What is a Living Wage? How should it be calculated? What is its relationship to the legal minimum wage? We assessed wages against recognized wage and poverty benchmarks and looked at whether take-home pay met workers' basic needs.

---

[62] ILO (2011) 'Freedom of Association and Development', Geneva: ILO

[63] ILO Conventions 87 and 98; ILO Declaration on fundamental principles and rights at work. In the MNE Declaration (art. 48, 49, 50, 51 and 52) the specific obligations of enterprises are described.

3. **Working hours:** Workers often have to work overtime to earn a decent wage and employers rely on overtime to achieve production targets. Where excessive working hours were found, Oxfam looked at why this was happening and the consequences of efforts by Unilever to ensure its suppliers complied with legal requirements.

4. **Contract labor:** Forms of contract labor, including temporary and seasonal work, are problematic because workers' livelihoods are precarious, causing them to live with insecurity and worry. Precarious work is a major concern to civil society organizations because people who are fearful of losing their jobs are unlikely to speak out or assert their rights. The study looked at why jobs are contracted on a precarious basis and the impact of this on workers' well-being.

Viet Nam was selected as the country case study for this report. Unilever Viet Nam (UVN) directly employs around 1,500 people producing home, personal care and food products. Oxfam's development and advocacy program in Viet Nam is well-established and includes a labor rights focus. Viet Nam is one of the world's fastest growing emerging economies and is currently undergoing a rapid transition from a centralized planned economy to a free market model, though one where the government still plays a major role. Food prices have risen significantly in recent years and there is currently a debate about the necessity for higher minimum wages and about the treatment of workers in general.

To ensure the study has wider relevance for Unilever and other companies, Oxfam looked at a range of international frameworks relevant for labor rights, in particular the **UN Guiding Principles on Business and Human Rights (UNGP)**, which guide companies in meeting their responsibilities to respect human rights. The principles are divided into four main elements[64]:

1. Commitment;
2. Integration of the policies in the business and implementation with suppliers;
3. Tools and processes for due diligence;
4. Remediation *via* grievance mechanisms.

---

[64] UN Guiding Principle 15

4. METHODOLOGY

Oxfam designed the study in ways that would enable it to assess how far people were able to realize their rights and whether the company's policies and processes help them to do so.

The study had both a global and national scope. Oxfam established global and Viet Nam-based research teams with expertise in labor standards within business. Unilever designated staff members from its global and Viet Nam bases to work with the research teams, providing information and access, and discussing findings. A UK consultancy was commissioned to develop a 'wage ladder' for Viet Nam with appropriate benchmarks for the location of Unilever's factory. Oxfam studied UVN and its supply chain within the country, to take into account a range of external and internal factors influencing labor standards. The researchers visited Unilever's operations at Cu Chi, near Ho Chi Minh City, where 700 workers were directly employed by Unilever and 800 more were employed by a labor provider to carry out simple processes, such as packing and cleaning. Managers and workers were interviewed. Worker interviews were a mix of individual and group formats, both on-site and off-site. The research team conducted telephone interviews with 48 of Unilever's Vietnamese suppliers, selected as being in a high-risk environment for labor standards, but where Unilever was judged to have commercial leverage based on information from UVN. From these 48 suppliers the researchers identified a representative spread of three suppliers, referred to in this report as selected or 'deep-dive' suppliers. One was a third-party manufacturer supplying a personal care product, one supplied plastic packaging and one supplied paper packaging. One was privately owned, one state-owned and one foreign-owned. The three suppliers were visited and interviews conducted with managers and workers using a similar format to the one used in Unilever's factory. Findings in the report have been anonymized.

5. FINDINGS RELATING TO UNILEVER'S POLICIES AND MANAGEMENT PROCESSES

Commitment

- Unilever has made a commitment to social responsibility by adopting the UNGP. It also has a Code of Business Principles (CoBP); a

Respect, Dignity and Fair Treatment policy; and a Supplier Code, all publicly stated.

- Despite this, human and labor rights are conspicuous by their absence from the Unilever Sustainable Living Plan. Social targets focus on the well-being of consumers and smallholders, but there are no targets for labor rights.

Integration of Labour Standards into the Business and Implementation with Suppliers

- Unilever management in Viet Nam were found to lack the capacity and knowledge to ensure the company's operations comply with international standards, nor did they have the authority to support suppliers to do so.
- Unilever is a valued client of its third-party manufacturers and suppliers in Viet Nam. However, in relation to labor rights many suppliers were unclear about Unilever's expectations and how best to realize labor rights in practice.
- Some Unilever sourcing practices were found to contribute to excessive working hours and precarious work in the supply chain.

Tools and Processes for due Diligence

- The risk management system, involving self-assessment and audit, is not sensitive to the vulnerability of some workers. Therefore none of the Vietnamese suppliers was identified as high risk through the risk assessment process.
- It is positive that the company will give time for improvements if problems are found; suppliers need to know this is the case and to understand the standards better.
- There are no tracking or internal reporting mechanisms covering Unilever's effectiveness in dealing with labor issues; input is not sought on this from civil society stakeholders.
- While Unilever shows a good level of transparency and actively engages with stakeholders at the global level, in Viet Nam this is at an early stage.

Remediation via Grievance Mechanisms

- Grievance mechanisms in Unilever's operations are ineffective because workers lack the confidence to use them, as a result of which potentially severe violations could be missed.
- Based on the phone survey, one in eight suppliers said workers do not have any grievances and a mechanism was not needed; only one in four have an assigned person and procedures to deal with them.

6. FINDINGS AT EACH LEVEL RELATING TO THE FOUR FOCUS ISSUES

The study looked at three levels of operations: Unilever global, Unilever Viet Nam and the supply chain in Viet Nam. For each, it came up with findings based on the four focus issues:

- Freedom of association and collective bargaining;
- Wages;
- Working hours; and
- Contract labour.

The below explores the key findings for each of these four focus issues at each level.

a. Global Level

Corporate policy appears to provide a good overall framework for these rights. The challenges arise when it comes to implementation, since the industrial relations policy of Unilever (and potentially other multinational corporations) may be country-specific and locally determined[65].

Commitment has been demonstrated by the actions taken to resolve industrial relations disputes and by Unilever's subsequent corporate engagement with the International Union of Food workers (IUF). This followed four complaints to the UK National Contact Point (NCP) responsible

---

[65] N. Dalton (2011) Vice President HR Global Supply Chain – Unilever, in interview with Oxfam on 15 September 2011.

for the OECD Guidelines on Multinational Enterprises, concerning violations of trade union rights[66]. In June 2012, the IUF lodged a further complaint with the UK NCP, alleging non-implementation by Unilever of the agreement reached in 2010 concerning the Doom Dooma factory in Assam, India manufacturing personal care products[67].

The Code of Business Principles (CoBP) includes a commitment to comply with all applicable laws on compensation, including minimum wage. Good practice codes (such as the ETI Base Code and SA8000) incorporate a commitment to a Living Wage.

The CoBP also includes a commitment to meet applicable national limits on working hours. National laws are frequently good in this area, but compliance is hard to achieve in a context of low wages.

Terminology in the CoBP assumes that all workers are in an employment relationship; it does not make it explicit that workers' rights are respected in the supply chain irrespective of employment status, although this was reported to be the intent. Good practice codes (such as the ETI Base Code and SA8000) use the term 'workers' to separate rights from employment status and include a commitment to Regular or Stable Employment.

b. Unilever Viet Nam Level

There is a UVN union but employees below management level do not have opportunities to raise issues collectively with management and have no meaningful involvement in collective bargaining. More could be done within the constraints of Viet Nam law to encourage an environment in which industrial relations can develop. This is likely also to be the case in other countries in which freedom of association is restricted by law.

The study found that all wages paid in Unilever's own factory clearly were well in excess of the applicable minimum wage, so were compliant with national law and Unilever policy. They also exceeded the international poverty line of $2 per day (taking into account household size). However, they were

---

[66] These complaints concerned site closure (Sewri factory, India), freedom of association and collective bargaining (Doom Dooma factory, India), and the use of temporary and contracted labour at factories (Rahim Yar Khan and Khanewal, Pakistan). A further complaint was submitted by the Turkish transport union TUMTIS in 2008. See: Unilever (2011) 'Respecting Rights', http://www.unilever.com/sustainable-living/ourpeople/rights

[67] For more information o the complaint, visit: http://oecdwatch.org/news-en/iuf-files-complaint-against-unilever ; For more information on the resolution, visit: http://www.oecd.org/dataoecd/0/16/44478619.pdf

found not to meet other key benchmarks of the basic needs of employees and their families, such as the Asia Floor Wage (4 million VND) and Oxfam's estimate of monthly expenses for an adult with a child (5.42 million VND). In interviews, workers were in agreement that wages were insufficient to make savings or support dependants (see Section 6).

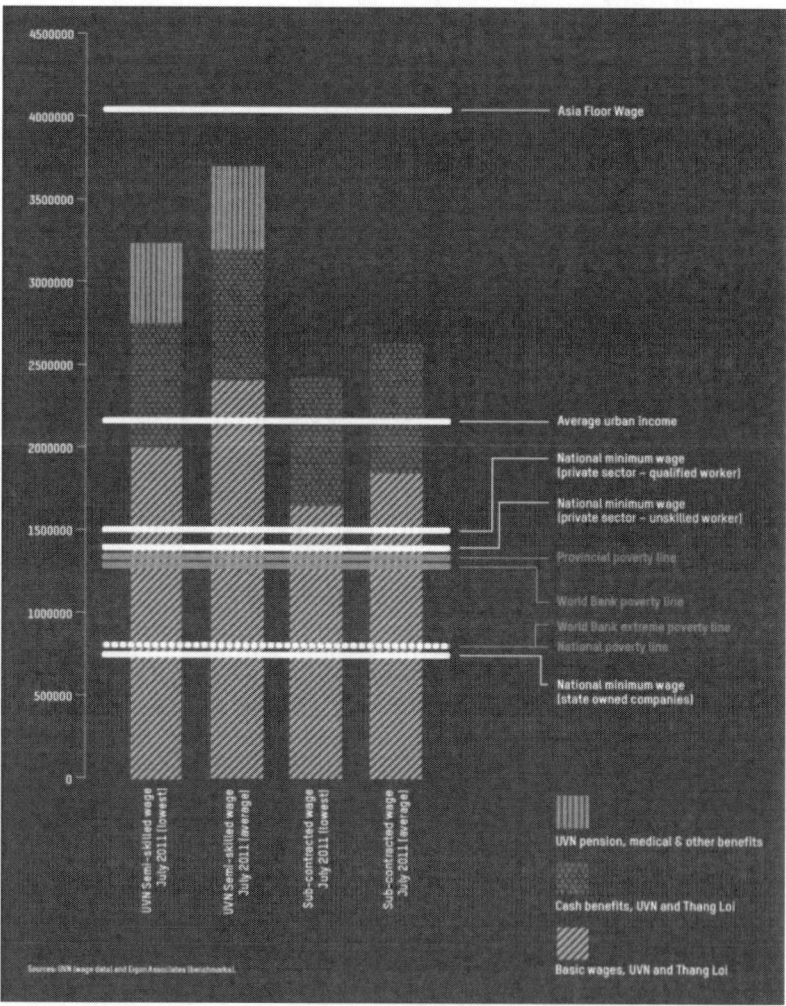

Sources: UVN (wage data) and Ergon Associates (benchmarks). Note that poverty and basic needs benchmarks relate to the needs of a household, not an individual.

Figure 3. Wages and benefits in Unilever Viet Nam (UVN) factory with wage and poverty benchmarks (Viet Nam Dong monthly, July 2011).

The Asia Floor Wage (AFW) benchmark was used as a reference point on the wage ladder because this methodology for calculating a Living Wage has the greatest currency amongst civil society organizations. Companies, including Unilever, therefore need to be aware how wages in their operations and key supply chain look in comparison to relevant AFW benchmarks.

The findings need to be put into a wider context of endemic low wages, reflected in a Fair Wage Network survey which found 25 per cent of workers in Viet Nam garment factories do not receive even the minimum wage (see Section 4). Nevertheless Oxfam concluded Unilever, as a profitable multinational corporation, could do more to ensure workers making their products can work their way out of poverty.

Unilever's working assumption at headquarters that production workers were paid well above a Living Wage in its own operations was not borne out by the study in Viet Nam and workers' perspective on wages and benefits was not found to be well understood by management.

Hours worked were found to be within legal limits and paid at a premium as required.

Just over half of the workers in the factory (748 out of 1,385) were sub-contracted to a labor provider, Thang Loi, rather than directly employed. These workers had lower wages and benefits than UVN employees; their average basic wages were still comfortably in excess of the legal minimum wage and the international poverty line, but less than half the AFW benchmark and Oxfam's estimate of workers' expenses (5.4 million VND). Some workers complained of unfair treatment and repeat temporary contracts.

Unilever has devised a Contingent Labor Reduction Roadmap to reduce the ratio of sub-contracted to directly employed workers where needed in a sustainable manner.

c. Viet Nam Supply Chain Level

Based on the phone survey, seven out of eight suppliers had a union, but one in two put workers outside the wage setting process. Three out of four regarded enterprise unions as more than a welfare body and approximately one in two saw them as providing an effective grievance handling mechanism.

Two of the three selected suppliers were found to pay a very low basic wage, just above the legal minimum. Unilever regularly checks that wages do meet the legal minimum; based on the Fair Wage Network survey[68], there are many enterprises in the garment and footwear sector that do not achieve this. In a supplier which had foreign ownership, Vietnamese managers and workers alike were unclear how wages were set.

Two of the selected suppliers were found to assume that offering overtime is necessary to retain workers. At one supplier, workers said they had worked four hours' overtime a day six days a week for ten months of the previous year: this is well in excess of legal limits of 200 hours a year. A social auditor had identified excessive working hours the previous year.

Thirty-two of the 48 suppliers surveyed by phone said they use temporary or sub-contracted workers; exploring the causes and impact of these was outside the scope of the study.

One supplier was found to have reduced its labor force to a minimum after the contract with Unilever was signed and managed fluctuations in demand by having a high ratio of temporary to permanent jobs. Since in Viet Nam only workers with contracts of more than six months can join the union, this is a significant barrier to workers having a collective voice about issues they are concerned about.

At one of the three 'deep-dive' suppliers, the research team found a range of good practices including higher wages (though not at the level of Oxfam's estimate of a Living Wage) and wage transparency. Low season was used to raise skills so workers could switch between tasks during busy periods meaning less reliance on temporary labor. Staff surveys and grievance mechanisms were trusted and used. Workers reported higher satisfaction than at the other suppliers or at Unilever's factory.

The fact that this supplier was managing to operate with better labor standards, in a similar high risk environment to the others studied, appeared to have no connection to the company's sourcing strategy.

7. ANALYSIS OF WHAT THE STUDY MEANS FOR UNILEVER

Unilever has made a significant commitment to social responsibility and sustainability; employees take pride in the company's values and a motivated workforce is seen as key to its business success.

---

[68] D. Vaughan-Whitehead (2011) 'How "fair" are wage practices along the supply chain? Global assessment in 2011-11', paper prepared for the Better Work conference, 26-28 October 2011, Washington DC, http://betterwork.org/global/?p=1296

"People must be the source of the company's value. Unilever must be best in class as we charge a premium for our brands, so we must invest in training and working conditions...We compete on operating efficiency, quality, specification of products and responsiveness to customer demand. All this requires an empowered and skilled workforce... All Unilever's analysis shows that where there are good conditions and empowerment of employees, the factory has the best results."

Nick Dalton, Unilever, VP HR Global Supply Chain[69]

Unilever's own analysis shows that the best results come from factories with good conditions and empowered workers; however, its business model does not fully reflect this. Based on this report, competitive advantage is still, in practice, pursued through downward pressure on labor costs, which pushes costs and risks onto workers.

Oxfam had expected to find endemic global supply chain issues, such as low wages, weak industrial relations and precarious work, within Unilever's 'high risk' suppliers, but were surprised to find them reported by workers in its own factory. We also found that workers, both in Unilever's factories and in its supply chain, had a weak voice and experienced 'inadvertent neglect'. We took it to be inadvertent as Unilever gives every sign of wanting to behave responsibly. However, it was clear that the workers experienced neglect, given the lack of a safe space to talking frankly about their concerns. This could mean that potentially severe labor violations do not come to the company's attention.

Demand for higher-quality standards and pressure on limited resources require smarter production and a more resilient and responsive supply chain from all companies. This in turn requires more skilled, efficient managers and workers who are open to innovation in the workplace. Unilever's control over its manufacturing operations and stable, long-term supply relationships make it well placed to deliver on this agenda.

Unilever now needs to incorporate the UNGP more fully into the way it runs its business, which will help it to ensure that those rights are realized. This will require the company to adopt a more people-centred approach, in which workers identify issues and priorities that matter most to them, give feedback on the quality of their working lives, and the effectiveness of

---

[69] N. Dalton (2011) Vice President HR Global Supply Chain – Unilever, in interview with Oxfam on 15 September 2011.

Unilever's mechanisms; as one stakeholder said in interview, 'it all starts with the workers'[70].

Proactive steps will be needed to address low wages and precarious work in the supply chain, to strengthen the due diligence process and to collaborate with other stakeholders, including competitors, civil society and governments. The implications of not addressing these concerns will be continued civil society criticism; difficulty in retaining skilled workers; and security of supply in the face of increasing competition for both.

Unilever needs to play a leadership role, while treating this as a 'pre-competitive' issue in which a range of other stakeholders – governments, civil society organizations, other companies – need to play their part.

8. OXFAM RECOMMENDATIONS TO UNILEVER

The below are recommendations developed by Oxfam for Unilever, based on the findings of the study. However, many of these recommendations would apply to many of Unilever's peers and competitors.

1. Adjust Policies and Business Model to Deliver Better Quality Jobs for Workers

- Change corporate policies (the Code of Business Principles and the Supplier Code) to build in a commitment to a Living Wage and minimise precarious work in Unilever's operations and supply chain.
- Acknowledge that the minimum wage is not always an adequate proxy for the basic needs of workers and their families.
- Identify and address low wages and precarious work in Unilever's operations and key supply chain.
- Move to a position where Unilever will source only from suppliers with good HR management, industrial relations and grievance mechanisms.
- Ensure any certification scheme with which Unilever is associated effectively enables the realisation of labour rights.

---

[70] D. Rees (2011) Director - ILO Better Work programme, in interview with Oxfam on 17 November 2011.

- Select strategic supply chains and work with competitors and other stakeholders to improve job quality (for instance, the tea industry).

2. Better Align Business Processes with Policy

- Introduce tools to support the strategy including:
- Training for buyers to understand the impact of their decisions on working hours, low wages and precarious work in the supply chain;
- Measurable targets for buyers to place an increasing value of orders with suppliers who are proactive in raising labour standards;
- Incentives for suppliers who are proactive in raising labour standards.
- Implement, alone or with industry peers (*e.g.* via AIM-Progress), a training programme for business partners and key suppliers at country level, addressing specific local issues relating to labour standards.
- Communicate expectations more clearly to suppliers, making clear where Unilever will take a continuous improvement approach, contingent on the supplier being transparent.
- Make better use of the knowledge of Unilever staff in-country about good practice in local conditions and provide guidance in the promotion of international standards, as well as compliance with national law.

3. Strengthen the Supply Chain due Diligence Process for Supply Chain Monitoring to Take Account of People's Vulnerability to Speak out

- Modify the risk management system to make it more sensitive to the situation of vulnerable workers, such as women with family responsibilities, migrants and those in precarious work, and rate as high-risk those countries which place limitations on freedom of association.
- Monitor the effectiveness of measures taken to address negative impact where identified and seek feedback from civil society organisations at country level.

- Bring local grievance processes into line with best practice based on the UNGP of being legitimate, accessible, predictable, equitable, rights-compatible and transparent.
- Recognize that a commercial audit programme, while necessary in an environment of poor legal compliance, is not sufficient for the realization of rights and needs to be strengthened by other mechanisms:
- Commission additional off-site worker interviews (*e.g.* conducted by NGOs) for sites which are 'high risk' and strategic;
- Specify a higher level of competence/training for third-party auditors
- Require auditors to assess wages against a credible basket of needs;
- Supplement audits with other mechanisms such as anonymous worker surveys, assessment of Human Resource Management, records of grievances raised and resolved, and frequency of negotiation of a Collective Bargaining Agreement.

4. Work with Others to Promote Scalable Ways to Realize Rights and Increase Collective Leverage

- Where Unilever has influence within its own business and over suppliers, it should encourage an environment in which industrial relations can develop and there can be bargaining on wages and benefits.
- Use Unilever's influence with governments to advocate that legal minima are adequate for basic needs, and to promote public/private strategies for social and economic upgrading.
- Consider joining a multi-stakeholder initiative such as the ETI to gain access to best practice know-how and approaches and opportunities to collaborate with others to address difficult issues.
- Write a progress report against Oxfam recommendations and Unilever commitments within two years, and enable Oxfam Viet Nam to check what has changed, particularly from workers' perspectives, in that time. Ensure responsibility is assigned internally to this.

5. Five Things Unilever Could Do in Viet Nam

- Share the findings of this study with managers, suppliers, the Viet Nam General Confederation of Labour and Cu Chi workers and pilot in Viet Nam the changes recommended in this report.
- Implement changes in ways of working at the Cu Chi factory. This should include regular meetings between management and workers; worker surveys; worker input into performance review processes; and understanding causes of underperformance.
- Review the ratio of directly employed to sub-contracted workers, employ those involved in production and packing directly, and address grievances about unfair treatment between UVN and Thang Loi employees.
- Take a closer look at standards in the 32 suppliers who reported using temporary and contract labour on production and packing lines, and change sourcing and contracting processes to deliver more open-ended jobs and wages that progress to a Living Wage.
- Provide more training and guidance to UVN managers to understand international standards and make better use of their knowledge in the audit programme and supplier management and development.

6. Integrate into the Sustainable Living Plan and/or Public Reporting Process Measurable Targets for Labour Rights and Job Quality

- Unilever must incorporate measures of labour rights and job quality into its public reporting processes so that stakeholders can assess its progress in managing the issues highlighted in this report. The principles and indicators developed for this study provide a useful tool for companies to assess their performance.
- Wage levels for a standard working week relative to the minimum wage, the international poverty line and the best available estimate of a Living Wage;
- Ratio of permanent to temporary contracts;
- Percentage of workers with an employment contract;
- Percentage of workers covered by a recent collective bargaining agreement;

- Number of significant grievances raised by workers and resolved by management;
- Awareness of workers' rights by workers and their supervisors (based on a survey).

CONCLUSION

Labor rights in supply chains have been an issue in global supply chains for decades. This study shows that the fast moving consumer goods industry continues to experience difficulties in improving working conditions in workplaces linked to its business in developing countries. The labor issues found in this study were broadly consistent with Oxfam's expectations. They are endemic issues in global supply chains, such as weak industrial relations, precarious work and wages being too low to meet basic needs (even where legally compliant). Unilever has made a top-level commitment to sustainability and social responsibility. It has the kind of corporate culture and long-term relationships with suppliers that make it ideally placed to sustain good-quality jobs in its operations and supply chain, if it is willing to make the necessary changes to its policies and processes and work collaboratively to address the root causes of labor problems. This would place Unilever in a potentially leading position to achieve the UNGP, which provide a clear road map to respecting human rights in the twenty-first century.

The lessons from this study are by no means uniquely focused on Unilever. They are important for the challenges faced by all global companies sourcing from developing countries. For these global companies to retain the trust of consumers, they must demonstrate a commitment to improving the lives of the poorest people connected to their business, often workers in their supply chains. They have the power to influence their suppliers and the resources and sophistication to adapt their approaches to local settings. However, it starts with the will to focus on the issue of labor rights over the longer term.

REFERENCES

Ethical Trading Initiative (2012). *ETI Base Code*. http://www.ethicaltrade.org/resources/key-eti-resources/eti-base-code.

Ethical Trading Initiative (2012). *ETI Management Benchmarks*. http://www. ethicaltrade.org/resources/key-eti-resources/eti-management-benchmarks.

Global Reporting Initiative (2011). *Sustainable Reporting Guidelines: version 3.1*. Amsterdam: Global Reporting Initiative, https://www. globalreporting.org/resourcelibrary/G3.1-Guidelines-Incl-Technical-Protocol.pdf.

International Labor Organization. *Database of International Labour Standards*. http://www.ilo.org/ilolex/english/convdisp1.htm.

International Labor Organization's webpage of publications, http://www.ilo. org/declaration/info/publications/lang--en/index.htm.

International Organization for Standardization (2010). *ISO 26000: Guidance on social responsibility*. Geneva: ISO, https://www.iso.org/obp/ui/# iso:std:iso:26000:ed-1:v1:en.

Ministry of Planning and Investment (2002). *Vietnamese Labour Code 23: Labour Code of Social Republic of Viet Nam*. Vietnamese Labour Code 23 June 1994, as amended 2 April 2002. Hanoi: National Assembly of the Republic of Viet Nam, http://www.global-standards.com/Resources/ VNLaborCode1994-2002.pdf.

Organisation for Economic Co-operation and Development (2011). *OECD Guidelines for Multinational Enterprises*. Paris: OECD Publishing, http://www.oecd.org/daf/internationalinvestment/guidelinesformultination alenterprises/48004323.pdf.

Ruggie, J. (2008). *Protect, Respect and Remedy: a Framework for Business and Human Rights*. A/HRC/8/5. Geneva: UN Human Rights Council. http://www.reports-and-materials.org/Ruggie-report-7-Apr-2008.pdf.

Ruggie, J. (2011). *UN Guiding Principles on Human Rights and Business: Implementing the United Nations 'Protect, Respect and Remedy'*. A/HRC/17/31. Geneva: UN Human Rights Council, http://www.business-humanrights.org/media/documents/ruggie/ruggie-guiding-principles-21-mar-2011.pdf.

UN Global Compact (2012). *The Ten Principles*. New York: UN Global Compact, http://www.unglobalcompact.org/aboutthegc/thetenprinciples/ index.html.

UN Global Compact. *Self Assessment Tool*. http://www. globalcompactself assessment.org/.

In: Multinational's CSR Practices …   ISBN: 978-1-63463-479-3
Editor: Alidou Ouedraogo   © 2015 Nova Science Publishers, Inc.

Chapter 8

MNCS IN BANGLADESH: ADDING VALUE THROUGH CSR

M. Babar
BizCare, Bangladesh

From climate change impacts to abuses of labor practices; from air and water pollution to forest depletion; from increased obesity to growing work-life imbalance; all fingers are pointed at business. More importantly, it is the private sector business which receives the brunt of this blame. Why not?

Though the governments, more broadly in the developing economies, have often been blamed for their inefficient policies, practices and policing, the private sector business, despite contributing one third of the global GDP, has been criticized vehemently. Worldwide, private sector owns or deals with a vast segment of the natural resources; produces and innovates more than half of the products; and employs about 40 per cent of the global population. So, it is obvious that they will be bracketed as being responsible for all the disarrays causing human loss or sufferings.

A glaring example of this inconvenient truth is the series of industrial disasters in Bangladesh. In late April this year (2013), collapse of a nine storied commercial building near the Bangladesh capital Dhaka created headline stories around the world. The incident killed over one thousand young workers who worked in several garment factories which were located in that ill-fated building. Thousands more were maimed and the survivors would certainly lead the rest of their lives highly traumatized. As it was not the only such incident in Bangladesh, the tragedy once again sparked instant debate about the responsibility of the business, regulators, government and all other stakeholders.

While eyebrows were raised at the owners and management of the factories who literally forced the workers to work in a premise that already loomed in active danger following visible cracks and ignoring advice of the local authorities to abandon the building before the accident, concerns brewed world-wide at the fragility of health and safety conditions at workplaces in this country. It was a question of moral obligation of the owners and the management of the garment factories to ensure safety of the workers, mostly poor women, who toil for several hours every day at the cheapest wages on earth to produce clothes for many global brands. The questions of irresponsibility thus go beyond and touch the reputed business houses everywhere, whether they are in the developed or developing blocs.

The industrial tragedies in Bangladesh or elsewhere clearly speak of the gaps in the value chain. Bangladesh and alike, emerging economies largely depend on extensive foreign direct investment with which flows in good practices of management, production and distribution. Globalization and free market economy have obviously facilitated such inroads paving unprecedented opportunities for the multinational or transnational companies. However, the main points of their attractions remained the availability of lower cost of production, marketing opportunities due to population concentration and other infrastructural support including energy. The underlying consideration was of course the massively growing appetite of the emerging economies to receive as much foreign investment and technology transfer. So, the private sector business seized the opportunity in full gear. The problem was that check and balance between the donor and the recipient was not in place in many instances. For a country like Bangladesh, ridden with poverty, it has been a crying need to seek as much foreign investment and technology and as such there have been huge compromises with agreeable standards which ultimately result in incidents like factory building collapse or fire or water pollution.

Bangladesh is a small country with a high population and scarce natural resources. Poverty looms large but corruption and bad governance pull down all holistic efforts to gear socio economic development. Though it is the major responsibility of the government, the private sector has successfully contributed much to the wellbeing of the people over the decades. The private sector became more active in being a development partner particularly in the wake of globalization and adoption of economic liberalization.

While scare resources, lack of technical knowhow and dearth of proper political will were the hindrances for engineering socio economic development, those were also the opportunities which were timely exploited by the private sector. Again, the lack of appropriate managerial and technical expertise in the domestic private sector coupled with the facility of globalization also made the inroad of multinational companies in Bangladesh.

The multinational companies started coming into Bangladesh during the late seventies. Definitely they came in with advanced administrative and technical capacity which helped in raising the standard of living in this country. However, their entry coincided with the rise of consumer interest that spanned from acceptable labor rights to ethical production to conservation of nature. These enforced the engagement of Corporate Social Responsibility.

Truly, Corporate Social Responsibility (CSR) has been in practice in this part of the world since a long period of time. However, those were more in the form of philanthropic concept. The philanthropic concept was mainly geared by religious and philosophical precepts. With the population of the region mostly being Muslims and Hindus, there was substantial adherence to these two religions. While Islam preaches alms giving like zakat, the well to do persons in the society indulged in extensive donations or charities. For Hinduism too, the stress was on Vedanta which ensured transparency and good conduct & governance. Being dominant, these two religions strongly influenced people's life and behavior in the region. Interestingly, such thoughts and practices have close resonance to the principles of what we call today as social responsibility.

Since the beginning of British colonial era, few local entrepreneurs had set up several establishments which were of course limited to schools, hospitals or clinics and places of worship. However, with the passage of time CSR started taking its weight following media blitz on 'irrational' behavior by certain reputed international companies in respect of reports like damage to environment, use of child labor etc.

The MNCs in Bangladesh have been driving the CSR renaissance in a spirit of adding value to their missions. In the backdrop of growing competitiveness and more importantly, in the wake of watchdog alertness of civil societies, media and consumers, MNCs tend to be in the quest of proving themselves as good and acceptable citizens. This, they believe, is imperative to safeguard their investment. Thus, CSR by MNCs represent the integrity with which they govern themselves, engage with the stakeholders and continuously measure and report their activities. In all count, they try to ensure and enhance their legitimacy. Companies are thus expected to perform well in non-financial areas such as human rights, business ethics, environmental policies, corporate contributions, community development, corporate governance, and workplace issues.

MNCs in Bangladesh, as elsewhere in the developing world, have conceived CSR as an opportunity to deliver effective solutions to several societal needs. These needs vary from basic provisions like housing, food, healthcare to education, employment, capacity building and co-hosting governmental actions for alleviation of poverty. Some MNCs have been engaged in broader aspects like ensuring workers health and safety, minimizing impacts on environment etc.

According to the UN Global Compact, the role of MNCs in development lies in their potentials to address social challenges through global partnerships and cooperation. However, the achievement of the Millennium Development Goals which map out eight key goals in poverty alleviation look to fall short and if anything, many of the issues not only persist but have become worse. Some have questioned the CSR agenda itself, which is largely reflective of Northern values and is predicated on a bias for voluntary mechanisms and a structural framework of robust social institutions such as rule of law and an independent media. Others have pointed to the persistence of global inequalities and have called for the re-conceptualization of CSR as oriented more explicitly towards global corporate citizenship.

While poverty alleviation remains the core developmental need in Bangladesh, many MNCs have chalked out their CSR strategies and activities accordingly. They may not have any direct intervention in helping to reduce the poverty scenario; their CSR activities go a long way to be effective in this regard. Interestingly, the MNCs in Bangladesh have responded to the local needs and not as much on prescriptions from outside. Of course, through their CSR activities the MNCs have been able to create or strengthen brand equity but at the end of the day, a greater help has been done to the poor people in this country. Unilever, for example, has programs on health, nutrition and hygiene which are in strong adherence to their core business and at the same time contributing to the achievement of some key MDGs.

With the rapid and revolutionary development in the domain of telecommunications, a new era is in place to propel progress and prosperity everywhere. At the same time, mobile phones are helping development of transparency, checking corruption and enabling common people to avail a plethora of public services including banking transactions at their doorsteps. Almost all mobile phone operators in Bangladesh are multinationals and therefore, besides bringing in massive investment, they have also brought in remarkable good management, skills and technology. As these companies generate huge financial incomes and more importantly for their competitive advantages, they have broad-based CSR programs which range from heritage preservation to improving ICT education to facilitating entrepreneurship development.

Initially the mobile phone companies have been practicing Responsive CSR which meant participating in sponsoring socio cultural and sporting events, donating to humanitarian causes etc. However, with the passage of time, some of the companies have redefined their CSR programs and are now following Strategic CSR which stresses more on sustainability.

Robi Axiata Limited, a subsidiary of the Malaysian Axiata Group and Japanese DoCoMo, for instance, now engages itself in providing computer skill development opportunities to young men and women in the rural areas. Under its ICT for Education program, it has provided computers to dozens of colleges in remote areas. More interestingly, it sends out its employees to train the students in those colleges with basic computer skills. Besides, Robi has also set up internet kiosks at the public libraries of all major cities across Bangladesh which allows common people to have access to the global information highway.

Added to the above mentioned program, Robi has also been providing home solar systems to hundreds of villagers in the off-grid regions of Bangladesh. This program is enabling the rural households to refrain from burning kerosene oil to light up homes in the evening thus lessening their carbon footprints. Also, in response to the regulator's prescription, the company is using solar energy at many of the base transmission station towers across the country. All these speak of their environmental stewardship, an important cornerstone of corporate social responsibility.

Likewise, another leading mobile phone company in Bangladesh, Grameenphone has been well known for their extensive CSR activities. Being a subsidiary of the global brand Telenor, Grameenphone's CSR activities mainly concentrate on developing ICT skills among children; empower common people with facilities to use mobile phone for basic or emergency health services etc. Though Grameenphone has integrated their mobile business with societal needs, they have enabled the people living in remote areas to be connected to the forum of health advices or distant education. This is also helping reduce the digital divide.

The oil and gas company Chevron has its involvement in activities for conservation of nature besides creating educational opportunities for the communities near their operations. Nestle Bangladesh has been doing extraordinary works in water conservation. Their initiatives involve recycling, rainwater harvesting and providing pure drinking water. Truly, these are the areas of greatest concern in Bangladesh. International banks like HSBC and Standard Chartered have also been piloting series of CSR programs aimed meeting some immediate needs of the people as well as creating opportunities for sustainable development of the local communities.

In all count, multinationals have proven that to be successful and sustainable, a business has to win the hearts, not the minds. In the past, entrepreneurs won the hearts by being philanthropic and charitable. However, today they have to be accountable with good governance and showing a visible difference in respecting human rights, improving lifestyle and safeguarding environment. In the context growing competitiveness in business, both from global as well as local perspective, it could be hard-edged decisions of the MNCs to design and implement effective CSR programs not because it is a nice thing to do but because it is imperative for good business. Impact of their conduct in Bangladesh can be felt anywhere in the world as already heeded by several globally reputed companies after the tragic events of garments industries near Dhaka recently.

While the MNCs in Bangladesh, like in many other countries, are contributing to socio economic development, they are pursuing their CSR policies with four justifications--- moral obligation, sustainability, license to operate and reputation management. It is true that the moral obligation of the MNCs have been embedded in their strategy not by its own will but more so because of the growing pressure and interest of the various stakeholders. In the backdrop of several incidents of irresponsible behavior by many reputed companies like Worldtel, Enron, Shell, Nike etc. in matters like financial manipulations to child labor to creating environmental hazards, MNCs have become alert to operate within law and respecting regulations. MNCs have also realized that sustainability depends on ensuring triple-bottom line (social, economic and environmental) approach. This means they have to secure operational activities with long term performance goals and avoid short term economic benefits or wasteful environmental uses. The license to operate has a deeper significance as it demands continuous dialogue with the local community and safeguarding their socio economic and environmental interests. Besides, dialogue with the stakeholders is also important for securing the license to operate. The Asian Energy, a British coal mining MNC, failed to operate in Bangladesh as they disregarded any dialogue with the local community with regard to the environmental and health safety issues. Reputation management is like an insurance. Companies pursue different social development activities to buy in the support and sympathy of the stakeholders in case of any untoward or unexpected incident. MNCs have taken due lessons from the Union Carbide chemical leak fall out in India in 1984. Despite pouring in millions of dollars in compensation, the Union Carbide authorities failed to reopen their factory.

The presence of MNCs operating in Bangladesh is obviously promoting the practice of CSR. At the same time, they are also motivating local industries and SMEs in particular, to follow ethical and sustainable business practices. MNCs also have the capacity to provide technical and financial support to non-governmental organizations. MNCs have helped lead the drive towards the practice of CSR. Being the major engine of growth, MNCs are the biggest tax payers and employment generators. Leaving aside the gaps that trigger industrial mishaps or other disorders, MNCs in Bangladesh are not only pushing ahead the economic growth but adding value to the overall societal progress as well. Leading the private sector business in this country they have been successful in proving they are aptly responsive to the mitigation if not eradication of many of the disarrays. In the face of unprecedented development of communication and information technology as well as steep rise in stakeholder's microscopic interest, global business has had to not only tighten the belt but engage in activities that ensure good conduct. They had come to terms with the mantra that they can be successful and sustainable only if they worked in the broad interest of the society. Through their extensive CSR policies and practices, they have also attested the fact drawn by the Harvard Business School that CSR is not about how a company makes profit but it uses the profit.

As business needed to make positive and visible contribution to societal progress and wellness through social, environmental and economic impacts, business dominated by MNCs is rigorously following the path to ensure a win-win scenario amongst all concerned.

EDITOR'S CONTACT INFORMATION

Dr. Alidou Ouedraogo,
Professor of Management
University of Moncton
18, Antonine- Maillet Street
Moncton (NB) E1A 3E9 Canada
Tel: 506-858-4216
Email: Alidou.ouedraogo@umoncton.ca

INDEX

#

20th century, 8
21st century, 25, 45

A

abolition, 3
abstraction, 112
abuse, 89, 112, 140
access, 1, 16, 21, 51, 52, 67, 69, 71, 119,
    125, 144, 154, 163
accessibility, 70
accommodation, 121
accountability, 92, 111, 112, 114, 127
accounting, 120, 121
activism, 15
adaptation(s), 84, 109
adults, 22
advocacy, 143
Africa, 51, 67, 69, 74, 115, 139
age, 22, 72, 101
agencies, 125
agriculture, 49, 73, 141
alertness, 161
altruism, 26
anchoring, 81
anger, 54
apex, 82
appetite, 160

Arab world, 67, 72
Asia, 46, 48, 57, 69, 74, 101, 133, 139, 148,
    149
aspiration, 43
assault, 56
assessment, 107, 130, 150, 154
assimilation, 85
ATLAS, 60
atmosphere, 120
attachment, 8, 76
attitudes, 111, 122
audit(s), 95, 139, 145, 154, 155
Austria, vii, 99, 102
authenticity, 6
authority(s), 19, 25, 53, 54, 73, 76, 77, 122,
    145, 165
automobile(s), 69, 74, 81
autonomy, 21
aversion, 14
awareness, 53, 60, 94, 95, 125, 131

B

Bangladesh, vi, viii, 27, 159, 160, 161, 162,
    163, 164, 165
banking, 49, 78, 162
banks, 164
bargaining, 154
barriers, 19, 72, 129
barriers to entry, 19

base, 23, 31, 82, 86, 91, 129, 156, 163
basic education, 101
basic needs, 23, 142, 148, 152, 154, 156
batteries, 64
behaviors, 111
Beijing, 44
Belgium, 101
benchmarks, 142, 144, 148, 149, 157
benefits, 25, 57, 70, 92, 119, 123, 128, 130, 148, 149, 154, 164
bias, 32, 162
biodiversity, 1, 24, 131
biomass, 62, 66
blame, 159
boilers, 66
bonuses, 89
BOP, 38, 88
brand image, 126
Brazil, 46, 52, 70, 113
breeding, 132
bribes, 91, 95
Britain, viii
brothers, 59
brutality, 44
bureaucracy, 52, 93
burn, 66
business ethics, 12, 48, 55, 56, 57, 162
business model, 151
business partners, 95, 153
businesses, 15, 93, 117, 121, 123, 125, 127, 128, 133
buyers, 153
by-products, 119

C

campaigns, 139
capacity building, 162
capitalism, 47, 55, 108
carbon, 62, 65, 74, 131, 163
case study, 70, 79, 82, 83, 85, 138, 143
catastrophes, 11
certificate, 77
certification, 28, 31, 60, 61, 78, 152

challenges, 3, 21, 85, 91, 97, 106, 109, 110, 121, 141, 146, 156, 162
changing environment, 123
chaos, 52
charities, 117, 125, 131, 133, 161
chemical, 165
child labor, 3, 161, 164
children, 1, 22, 27, 76, 101, 163
China, 43, 44, 45, 46, 47, 48, 49, 50, 51, 52, 53, 54, 55, 56, 57, 131
Chinese firms, 50, 51, 54
Chinese government, 47, 50, 51, 53
circulation, 44
city(s), 2, 64, 144, 163
citizens, 44, 45, 54, 94
citizenship, 162
civil servants, 90
civil society, 23, 94, 97, 143, 145, 149, 152, 153
civilization, 55
clarity, 13, 118
classroom, 55
cleaning, 144
clients, 11, 20, 29, 64, 67, 99
climate, 24, 73, 80, 103, 159
climate change, 80, 159
close relationships, 93
closure, 147
clusters, 131
CO_2, 1, 62, 63, 64, 65, 66, 79, 80
CO_2 emissions, 1, 62, 64, 65, 80
coal, 120, 121, 130, 164
codes, 97, 108, 111, 139
codes of conduct, 97, 108, 111, 139
coherence, 77
collaboration, 24, 51, 59, 70, 81, 96, 131, 141
collective bargaining, 3, 142, 146, 147, 155
colleges, 163
collusion, 55, 89, 90
commerce, 29
commercial(s), 6, 8, 13, 26, 29, 59, 68, 85, 90, 96, 99, 120, 124, 129, 135, 144, 154, 159
common rule, 8, 96

common sense, 23
communication, 28, 31, 95, 126, 165
community(s), 8, 31, 47, 51, 53, 55, 69, 81,
    97, 102, 106, 107, 111, 122, 123, 125,
    127, 128, 129, 162, 163, 164
community support, 127
comparative advantage, 112
comparative analysis, 76
compensation, 147, 165
competition, 6, 29, 43, 73, 90, 93, 152
competitive advantage, 6, 19, 39, 73, 88,
    109, 118, 119, 127, 151, 163
competitiveness, 78, 124, 161, 164
competitors, 4, 138, 152, 153
complement, 64, 142
compliance, 3, 94, 97, 138, 139, 140, 141,
    147, 153, 154
composition, 77
compression, 63
computer, 49, 102, 163
computer skills, 163
conception, 56
conceptual model, 35
conceptualization, 13, 82, 162
conference, 1, 150
conflict, 14, 16, 52, 108
conflict of interest, 52
conformity, 3, 26, 29, 76, 77, 78, 79, 114
confrontation, 4
Confucius, 55
Congo, 56
Congress, 39
consciousness, 20
consensus, 6, 12, 29, 30, 32, 125
conservation, 61, 131, 132, 161, 163
Constitution, 78
construction, 4, 36, 60, 67, 77, 80, 85
consulting, 103
consumer goods, 49, 156
consumers, 5, 6, 16, 47, 49, 52, 53, 54, 71,
    111, 119, 121, 126, 137, 145, 156, 161
consumption, 45, 61, 62, 65, 130
containers, 72
content analysis, 38
contingency, 6, 127

controversial, 124, 130
controversies, 6, 18
convergence, 26, 80, 85
cooking, 65
cooperation, 84, 162
coordination, vii, 20, 108
corporate entities, 1, 2, 11
corporate fraud, 98
corporate governance, 89, 93, 162
corporate sector, 127
Corporate Social Responsibility (CSR), 3, 5,
    10, 12, 14, 17, 21, 32, 33, 34, 35, 37, 38,
    39, 40, 41, 87, 88, 94, 106, 113, 114,
    115, 134, 135, 161
correlation, 15
corruption, 2, 3, 4, 23, 29, 52, 53, 54, 55,
    89, 90, 91, 92, 93, 94, 95, 96, 97, 98,
    106, 108, 111, 160, 162
cost, 12, 18, 20, 67, 74, 75, 81, 91, 92, 102,
    104, 118, 119, 120, 127, 130, 160
cost accounting, 120
cost benefit analysis, 118
country of origin, 7
covering, 78, 145
cracks, 160
creativity, 45
credentials, 119
crises, 4, 5, 45, 71
criticism, 5, 26, 31, 32, 48, 54, 119, 125,
    152
CRM, 125
crops, 102
CSD, 120
cultivation, 124
cultural differences, 108
culture, 45, 47, 55, 57, 90, 95, 96, 97, 122,
    133, 141, 156
currency, 149
curriculum, 55
customer loyalty, 17
customers, 46, 75
cycles, 111
cycling, 131

D

Daewoo, 124
damages, 92, 94
danger, 110, 119, 160
database, 36
decentralization, 18
decision makers, 2, 25, 71
decision-making process, 108
Declaration on Fundamental Principles and
    Rights at Work, 2
decoupling, 114
deficiency(s), 55, 77, 84
delegates, 17
democracy, 23, 89, 103
demonstrations, 54
deontology, 49
depth, 139
deregulation, 105
designers, 30, 49, 50
detection, 29
developed countries, 12, 25, 27, 28, 31, 85,
    90
developing countries, vii, 4, 6, 7, 24, 25, 26,
    27, 28, 30, 75, 82, 83, 84, 85, 92, 93, 94,
    97, 98, 106, 107, 108, 109, 111, 112,
    135, 137, 138, 156
diabetes, 102
diesel fuel, 62
diffusion, 3
digital divide, 163
directives, 79, 108
directors, 9, 10, 17, 18, 95
disappointment, 139
disaster, 119, 132
discomfort, 93
discrimination, 3, 76, 78
discussion groups, 5
diseases, 53, 102
dissatisfaction, 121
distortions, 89, 92
distribution, 1, 18, 23, 24, 57, 122, 160
diversity, 5, 55, 69, 80, 107, 131, 134
doctors, 102, 127
donations, 8, 124, 131, 161

downsizing, 63
draft, 31
drawing, 46
dream, 9, 45, 47
drinking water, 164
duality, 110

E

East Asia, 131
ecological processes, 131
ecology, 37
economic activity, 117, 118
economic behaviour, 8
economic development, 7, 9, 13, 22, 77, 98,
    160, 161, 164
economic fundamentals, 71
economic growth, 11, 22, 23, 25, 53, 71, 89,
    137, 165
economic liberalization, 160
economic performance, 6, 12, 55
economic power, 43, 52
economic reform, 47
economic theory, 40
economic transformation, 44
economics, 13, 48, 84
economies in transition, 31
ecosystem, 118, 130, 131
education, 22, 23, 36, 57, 69, 80, 100, 101,
    107, 121, 133, 162, 163
educational opportunities, 163
effluents, 66
Egypt, 72
electricity, 62, 63, 80, 120, 121
emergency, 163
emerging markets, 51, 55
emission, 62, 64, 65, 66
emotional intelligence, 43
empirical studies, 5
employees, 11, 13, 46, 47, 48, 52, 69, 73,
    90, 92, 95, 102, 127, 128, 147, 148, 149,
    150, 151, 155, 163
employers, 143
employment, 3, 11, 68, 75, 139, 147, 155,
    162, 165

employment relationship, 147
employment status, 147
empowerment, 96, 151
encouragement, 27, 128
endangered, 100, 131
endangered species, 100, 131
energy, 61, 62, 65, 74, 75, 80, 96, 133, 160, 163
energy consumption, 61, 65, 75
enforcement, 53, 90, 92, 93, 111
engineering, 68, 161
England, 8, 44, 121
entrepreneurs, 12, 47, 48, 161, 164
entrepreneurship, 163
environment(s), 2, 4, 11, 18, 24, 28, 29, 33, 48, 53, 59, 60, 61, 62, 63, 64, 67, 77, 79, 80, 83, 94, 97, 106, 107, 110, 111, 112, 118, 120, 122, 125, 130, 132, 144, 147, 150, 154, 161, 162, 164
environmental aspects, 24
environmental conditions, 96, 106, 111
environmental crisis, 53
environmental factors, 28
environmental impact, 65, 80, 120
environmental issues, 21, 45, 53, 64, 95
environmental management, 30, 61, 120
environmental protection, 11, 53, 70, 77, 78, 83, 94, 131
environmental standards, 101
equal opportunity, 60, 69
equality, 1, 57, 76
equilibrium, 23, 24, 71, 84
equipment, 74, 103
equity, 57, 162
ethical implications, 122
ethical issues, 121
ethical values, 5, 48, 55
ethics, 16, 18, 21, 39, 48, 55, 95, 118, 121, 122
eucalyptus, 66, 80
Eurasia, 53
Europe, 4, 12, 44, 45, 46, 47, 50, 54, 66, 69, 71, 74, 100, 123
European Commission, 6, 12, 13
European market, 50

European Union (EU), 47, 62, 65, 72, 86, 101
evidence, 108, 121, 124, 128, 139
evil, 89
evolution, viii, 7, 9, 10, 12, 37, 64, 76
exercise, 32, 102, 103, 112, 130, 142
expertise, 30, 31, 67, 84, 96, 127, 137, 144, 161
exploitation, 7, 13, 22, 34, 47, 56, 87
exporters, 49
exports, 68
external environment, 129
external relations, 89
externalities, 48
extraction, 132
extreme poverty, 46

F

factories, 51, 139, 147, 149, 151, 159, 160
fair trade, 5, 24
fairness, 24, 95
faith, 111
families, 8, 13, 102, 128, 148, 152
fantasy, 47
farms, 121
fatalism, 85
fauna, 66
fear, 32, 54
financial, 4, 5, 12, 13, 15, 26, 41, 45, 46, 49, 63, 64, 71, 73, 76, 82, 88, 92, 95, 127, 129, 135, 161, 163, 164, 165
financial crisis, 45, 47, 71
financial markets, 73
financial performance, 5, 41, 82, 88, 135
financial records, 95
financial support, 165
firm value, 20
first generation, 63
fisheries, 73
floods, 49
fluctuations, 150
food, 27, 49, 78, 102, 138, 143, 162
food industry, 49
food products, 143

footwear, 150
force, 9, 16, 26, 29
Fordism, 11
foreign direct investment, 160
foreign firms, 85
foreign investment, 111, 160
formation, 56, 127
formula, 4
foundations, 45, 97
fragility, 160
framing, 30
France, vii, 1, 8, 33, 34, 35, 43, 44, 46, 62, 68, 69, 74, 87
franchise, 127
Franklin, Benjamin, 26
fraud, 29, 89
free market economy, 160
free trade, 71, 72
freedom, 3, 76, 147, 153
friction, 63
fruits, 127
fuel consumption, 63
fundamental needs, 22
funds, 95, 124, 126
future orientation, 3

G

GDP, 22, 71, 105, 159
GDP per capita, 22
gender equality, 23
gene pool, 131
General Motors, 120
Germany, 8, 44, 52, 54
gestures, 109
Gibraltar, 74
glasses, 102
Global Compact, 2, 3, 27, 28, 91, 98, 111, 157, 162
global economy, 44
global warming, 62, 133
globalization, 11, 15, 105, 106, 160, 161
goods and services, 137
governance, 18, 23, 25, 52, 55, 78, 97, 98, 111, 160, 161, 164

government spending, 124
governments, 6, 16, 25, 29, 90, 94, 97, 105, 106, 140, 141, 152, 154, 159
grants, 17, 21, 73, 83, 84
Great Britain, viii, 137
Greece, 39
greenhouse, 62, 65
greenhouse gas(s), 62, 65
greenhouse gas emissions, 62
grouping, 82
growth, 6, 7, 8, 15, 19, 28, 59, 71, 90, 97, 110, 127, 128, 137, 165
guidance, 93, 153, 155
guidelines, 30, 31, 111

H

habitat(s), 132
harmonization, 108
harmony, 83
harvesting, 164
Hawaii, 34
hazards, 164
health, 22, 23, 45, 54, 56, 57, 90, 102, 103, 120, 123, 131, 139, 160, 162, 163, 164
health care, 102, 103
health insurance, 57
health risks, 56
health services, 124, 163
hegemony, 32
higher education, 69, 132
hiring, 69, 75, 90
history, 8, 43, 44, 45, 52, 54, 122
homes, 47, 120, 163
honesty, 95
host, 4, 6, 70, 80, 82, 99, 107, 108, 109, 110
housing, 27, 121, 162
human, 1, 2, 3, 6, 7, 8, 18, 22, 23, 72, 75, 76, 78, 90, 93, 94, 95, 106, 108, 111, 119, 122, 125, 126, 138, 139, 143, 145, 156, 159, 162, 164
human activity, 122
human capital, 23
human development, 22, 23
Human Development Index, 22

Human Resource Management, 154
human resources, 72, 75
human right(s), 1, 2, 3, 6, 23, 76, 78, 90, 93, 94, 106, 108, 111, 125, 143, 156, 162, 164
human suffering, 2
hybrid, 14
hygiene, 162

I

icon, 126
ideal, 64
identification, 31, 57, 96
image, 6, 11, 27, 50, 53, 54, 57, 83, 100, 118, 119, 125, 126, 128
imitation, 19
immersion, 28
impact assessment, 129, 130
improvements, 77, 145
in transition, 29
inauguration, 85
income, 100, 101, 118
India, v, 46, 52, 61, 99, 100, 101, 103, 147, 165
indirect effect, 106
individual action, 92, 97
individualism, 9
individuals, vii, 1, 14, 16, 20, 47, 52, 55, 119, 124, 131
Indonesia, 131, 142
industrial relations, 141, 146, 147, 151, 152, 154, 156
industry(s), 9, 10, 11, 13, 14, 21, 41, 45, 50, 51, 61, 64, 67, 68, 83, 88, 91, 138, 142, 153, 156, 164, 165
inequality, 53, 55, 93, 109
inflation, 71
information technology, 165
infrastructure, 72, 83
injuries, 51
insecurity, 60, 143
institution building, 108
institutions, vii, 2, 6, 20, 23, 25, 46, 90, 93, 109, 111, 122

integration, 6, 13, 20, 23, 31, 64, 84, 94, 107, 112
integrity, 43, 92, 93, 95, 96, 97, 98, 161
intellectual property, 73
intellectual property rights, 73
interest groups, 73, 125
internal controls, 95
International Chamber of Commerce, 91
international standards, 60, 72, 78, 91, 140, 142, 145, 153, 155
international trade, 139
internationalization, 21
intervention, 117, 162
intrinsic value, 14
intrusions, 106
investment(s), 6, 26, 49, 51, 67, 68, 71, 73, 75, 80, 82, 85, 92, 93, 94, 103, 124, 137, 160, 161, 162
investors, 71, 72, 84, 92
Iran, 135
iron, 130
Islam, 161
isolation, 84, 132
issues, vii, 4, 8, 12, 37, 48, 50, 52, 53, 54, 78, 87, 89, 91, 94, 95, 97, 107, 108, 109, 118, 119, 123, 125, 138, 139, 140, 141, 142, 145, 146, 147, 150, 151, 153, 154, 155, 156, 162, 164
Italy, vii

J

Japan, 49, 52, 54
job creation, 68, 101
joint ventures, 44
Jordan, 72

K

kerosene, 163
kill, 100
Kyoto Protocol, 24

L

labor force, 51, 150
lack of control, 52
languages, 72
Latin America, 27, 139
laws, 8, 29, 47, 73, 77, 79, 80, 90, 92, 93, 147
laws and regulations, 29, 80, 93
leadership, 23, 43, 45, 46, 51, 52, 54, 55, 57, 90, 123, 152
learning, 109, 122
Lebanon, vii, 105
legislation, 77
lens, 41, 88, 114
level of education, 22
liberty, 23
LIFE, 63
life cycle, 60, 63
life expectancy, 22
light, 3, 6, 17, 18, 92, 93, 121, 163
liquids, 65, 66
living conditions, 47, 53
loans, 124
local authorities, 70, 129, 160
local community, 13, 106, 107, 123, 127, 164
local conditions, 32, 142, 153
local government, 96
logistics, viii, 73
loyalty, 41, 128
LPG, 62

M

majority, 23, 24, 45, 64, 107, 108, 138
Malaysia, vii, 117, 131, 132, 135
malnutrition, 22, 102
man, 1, 3, 76, 102, 165
manufacturing, 8, 50, 60, 62, 65, 66, 67, 73, 93, 139, 147, 151
market economy, 20, 23
market share, 19, 124
marketing, 92, 117, 119, 120, 123, 124, 125, 127, 160
marketplace, 75, 90
marriage, 135
mass, 54, 63, 64
materials, 63, 71, 157
matter, 15, 23, 29, 31, 91, 151
measure of value, 119
media, 16, 49, 53, 54, 60, 125, 126, 157, 161, 162
medicine, 102, 103
Mediterranean, 67, 71, 72, 74
mentoring, 81
meritocracy, 69
methodology, 4, 76, 149
Mexico, 108
microclimate, 131
middle class, 46
Middle East, 46
migrants, 153
Min, Ho Chi, 144
minimum wage(s), 139, 142, 143, 147, 149, 152, 155
mission(s), 63, 76, 82, 125, 126, 161
MNC, v, 6, 7, 84, 85, 105, 106, 107, 108, 109, 110, 111, 114, 115, 164
mobile phone, 162, 163
models, 6, 15, 47, 52, 56, 63, 64, 74, 108, 130
modernity, 122
momentum, 45
money laundering, 89
Moon, 56, 107, 115
morale, 92, 128
Morocco, v, 59, 61, 64, 66, 67, 68, 69, 70, 71, 72, 73, 74, 76, 78, 79, 80, 81, 82, 83, 85
mosaic, 62
motivation, 10, 45, 129
multinational companies, 4, 6, 7, 161
multinational corporations, 120, 146
multinational firms, 9
multiplication, 21
music, 133
Muslims, 101, 161

N

national culture, 46
national identity, 39
National Survey, 128, 134
nationalism, 56
nationality, 1
natural gas, 62
natural resources, 23, 51, 80, 159, 160
NCP, 146
negative consequences, 106
negative influences, 112
neglect, 151
negotiating, 5, 68
negotiation, 154
neoliberal dogmas, 4
neutral, 15
NGO(s), 2, 23, 51, 103, 123, 128, 130, 132,
    134, 141, 142, 154
Nigeria, 34, 86, 108, 113, 114
Nobel Prize, 103
North America, 4, 8, 46, 50, 74
nutrient, 131
nutrition, 162

O

obesity, 159
objectivity, 31, 32, 86, 119
obstacles, 25, 91, 93, 141
OECD, 6, 7, 90, 98, 147, 157
officials, 52
offshoring, 70
oil, 71, 83, 120, 130, 131, 132, 163
operations, 61, 90, 97, 105, 106, 111, 118,
    120, 121, 131, 132, 138, 140, 141, 142,
    144, 145, 146, 149, 151, 152, 156, 163
opportunities, 26, 70, 92, 112, 127, 132,
    147, 154, 160, 161, 163, 164
optimism, 28
optimization, 65
organism, 14, 16, 23
organize, viii
originality, 85

outreach, 133
outsourcing, 25, 83, 85
overtime, 143, 150
ownership, 21, 38, 96, 107, 108, 129, 132,
    150
ownership structure, 38

P

Pacific, 57
Pakistan, 147
participants, 1, 2, 11, 28
peace, 119
personality, 45
petroleum, 62, 132
pharmaceuticals, 130
plants, 59, 61, 62, 63, 66, 68
platform, 65, 67, 69, 71, 74, 91
playing, 92
pluralism, 9
police, 23, 104
policy, 60, 62, 69, 95, 122, 126, 134, 145,
    146, 147
political leaders, 54
political legitimacy, 57
political party, 94
political power, 55
political system, 105
polluters, 77
pollution, 53, 61, 64, 77, 79, 139, 159, 160
pools, 61, 66
population, 22, 23, 25, 37, 43, 53, 54, 55,
    68, 69, 72, 75, 81, 84, 128, 132, 159,
    160, 161
population size, 132
positive attitudes, 125
positive correlation, 82
poverty, 22, 24, 37, 53, 54, 93, 108, 109,
    111, 131, 137, 139, 142, 147, 148, 149,
    155, 160, 162
poverty alleviation, 108, 131, 162
poverty line, 22, 147, 149, 155
poverty reduction, 24
practical knowledge, 8
predators, 85

predictability, 94
premature death, 53
preparation, vii
preservation, 24, 163
President, 23
prevention, 24
principles, 2, 4, 11, 12, 21, 24, 28, 31, 77,
   78, 85, 90, 91, 93, 95, 98, 111, 118, 120,
   124, 133, 142, 143, 155, 157, 161
private sector, 8, 14, 30, 73, 89, 90, 91, 92,
   94, 96, 97, 98, 159, 160, 161, 165
privatization, 105
probability, 22
procurement, 92
producers, 101
production targets, 143
professionals, 29
profit, 4, 6, 11, 17, 26, 28, 35, 49, 69, 85,
   118, 121-125, 128, 129, 165
profitability, 26, 75, 82, 89, 118, 133
project, 27, 29, 30, 62, 63, 67, 68, 74, 75,
   80, 86, 125, 128, 130, 131, 142
proliferation, 10
propaganda, 15
property rights, 35, 93
prosperity, 45, 53, 162
protected areas, 100
protection, 3, 8, 76, 93, 111, 132, 140
protectionism, 7
public administration, 47
public investment, 71
public officials, 90
public opinion, 6, 92, 94, 97
public policy, 71, 96, 97
public sector, 7, 30, 96, 129
public service, 162
public-private partnerships, 52
publishing, 6

Q

quality control, 78
quality of life, 13
quality standards, 51, 66, 151
questioning, 31

R

race, 106
racing, 59
radius, 103
rating agencies, 13
rationality, 32
raw materials, 130
reactions, 51
reading, 43
reality, 3, 49, 86, 111
reasoning, 110
recall, 126
recognition, 3, 19, 47, 54, 65, 75, 122, 127,
   129
recommendations, 132, 152, 154
reconciliation, 27, 85
recovery, 5
recycling, 60, 62, 63, 164
redistribution, 55
regenerate, 56
regions of the world, 29
regulations, 19, 21, 79, 82, 94, 97, 101, 111,
   164
regulatory agencies, 52
regulatory framework, 7, 28, 77, 91
rehabilitation, 131, 132
relaxation, 79
relevance, vii, 143
reliability, 38, 54, 95
religion, 33, 101
religious beliefs, 85
religious traditions, 36, 55
renaissance, 161
renewable energy, 65, 120
repair, 7
repression, 54
reputation, 4, 45, 48, 49, 50, 53, 54, 92, 119,
   125, 133, 164
requirements, 11, 28, 66, 69, 76, 78, 80, 83,
   108, 122, 143
researchers, 5, 7, 8, 13, 16, 83, 85, 139, 144
resentment, 51
reserves, 95, 132
resistance, 3, 5, 20

resolution, 147
resource allocation, 111, 119
resource management, 18, 95
resources, 14, 19, 20, 22, 24, 25, 51, 52, 66, 74, 75, 79, 92, 105, 109, 110, 130, 132, 140, 151, 156, 157, 161
response, 50, 163
responsiveness, 46, 107, 151
restoration, 131
retail, 127
revenue, 1, 78
rewards, 92, 127, 128
rhetoric, 14, 112
rhino, 132
rhythm, 21, 69
rights, 2, 3, 6, 8, 18, 34, 76, 86, 134, 137, 138, 139, 140, 141, 142, 143, 144, 145, 146, 147, 151, 152, 154, 155, 156, 161
Rio Declaration on Environment and Development, 2
risk(s), 4, 24, 32, 48, 90, 92, 93, 94, 95, 100, 105, 106, 109, 112, 124, 142, 144, 145, 150, 151, 153, 154
risk assessment, 145
risk management, 145, 153
river systems, 132
Romania, 69, 70
root(s), 12, 18, 69, 85, 140, 156
routines, 19
Royal Society, 131
rule of law, 89, 141, 162
rules, 29, 79, 82, 94, 95
rural areas, 163
Russia, 44, 52, 57, 61

S

safety, 50, 52, 54, 90, 120, 160, 162, 164
Samsung, 59
Sarbanes-Oxley Act, 90
savings, 148
school, 55, 69, 81, 84, 102, 161
scope, 19, 25, 30, 63, 144, 150
Second World, 8, 45, 59
security, 30, 69, 78, 80, 102, 104, 152

security guard, 102, 104
self-assessment, 145
self-interest, 110
self-regulation, 91
seminars, 135
sensitivity, 11
sensitization, 10
services, 23, 29, 63, 64, 72, 73, 75, 78, 103, 124, 127, 131
shareholder value, 85
shareholders, 3, 4, 11, 14, 17, 26, 46, 47, 121, 123
shortage, 5
showing, 164
signals, 4, 28, 44, 47, 52
signs, 121, 133
skilled workers, 152
small businesses, 15
soccer, 62
social activities, 51
social audit, 139, 150
social behaviour, 19
social benefits, 25
social contract, 48, 56
social control, 109, 113
social development, 22, 89, 97, 165
social fabric, 7
social institutions, 162
social intangibles, 12
social justice, 55
social network, 52, 84
social problems, 84
social relations, 11, 78
social relationships, 11, 78
social structure, 19, 20
socialization, 20
society, 2, 4, 5, 8, 9, 10, 11, 13, 14, 16, 18, 27, 29, 31, 36, 45, 47, 48, 55, 56, 57, 60, 76, 81, 82, 85, 89, 90, 94, 97, 104, 117, 118, 119, 122, 124, 125, 127, 129, 130, 133, 152, 161, 165
sociology, 101
software, 50
solar system, 163
solidarity, 47

solution, 91
South Africa, 27
South America, 74
Spain, 69, 71, 74
species, 130, 131, 132
speculation, 46
spending, 71
spillover effects, 106
stability, 20
staff members, 144
stakeholder groups, 125
stakeholders, 3, 4, 30, 45, 46, 47, 48, 51,
    100, 107-110, 112, 118, 121, 123, 129,
    130, 145, 152, 153, 155, 160, 161, 164
standard of living, 161
standardization, 32, 77
state(s), 14, 19, 25, 47, 51, 52, 54, 55, 57,
    66, 67, 68, 79, 82, 85, 102, 105, 117,
    118, 122, 128, 144
stress, 161
structural reforms, 71
structure, 19, 52, 94, 95, 102, 103, 107, 111
structuring, 9
substitution, 19, 119
succession, 52
supervisor(s), 139, 156
supplier(s), 11, 20, 52, 63, 74, 90, 93, 95,
    96, 137-141, 143, 144, 145, 146, 149,
    150, 151, 152, 153, 154, 155, 156
supply chain, 93, 94, 95, 96, 97, 137-142,
    144-147, 149, 150, 151, 152, 153, 156
surveillance, 77
survival, 23, 120, 122, 132
survivors, 159
sustainability, 23, 48, 67, 84, 91, 111, 129,
    134, 135, 139, 150, 156, 163, 164
sustainable development, 12, 13, 22, 24, 28,
    34, 38, 55, 78, 86, 97, 113, 120, 134, 164
sustainable economic growth, 73
sympathy, 165

T

tangible benefits, 24
Tanzania, 115

target, 48, 62, 124, 125, 126
tariff, 72
taxation, 68, 70
taxes, 71, 74, 124
teams, 127, 144
technological progress, 29
technology(s), 51, 54, 61, 63, 65, 66, 70,
    119, 137, 160, 163
technology transfer, 160
telecommunications, 49, 162
telephone, 144
tensions, 47, 54, 108
territorial, 8
territory, 79
testing, 9
textbook, 40
theoretical approaches, 9
thermal energy, 65, 66, 74
thoughts, 161
threats, 89, 97
top-down, 139
toxic products, 43
toxic waste, 61
trade, 5, 24, 29, 44, 68, 125, 137, 140, 141,
    142, 147
trade union, 125, 140, 141, 142, 147
trainees, 73
training, 68, 69, 72, 73, 74, 75, 77, 80, 96,
    132, 151, 153, 154, 155
transactions, 162
transformation, 5, 47
translation, 11, 12
translocation, 132
transmission, 163
transparency, 3, 73, 91, 92, 96, 98, 111, 138,
    145, 150, 161, 162
transport, 69, 147
transportation, 81, 84
Treasury, 71
treaties, 24, 44, 78, 98
treatment, 66, 78, 143, 149, 155
triggers, 46, 47
Turkey, 69, 72
turnover, 60

U

UNDP, 22
Union Carbide, 165
unions, 23, 25, 149
United Kingdom (UK), vii, 36, 113, 114, 116, 117, 118, 120, 121, 123, 128, 131, 135, 144, 146
United Nations (UN), 1, 2, 11, 22, 28, 90, 91, 98, 111, 143, 157, 162
United Nations Convention against Corruption, 2, 28, 90, 98
United States, 24, 25, 47, 50, 52
Universal Declaration of Human Rights, 2
universality, 21
universities, 72, 78
urban, 51, 64
urban areas, 51
USA, 139

V

variables, 13, 15
vehicles, 59, 60, 62, 63, 64, 65, 66, 67, 83
ventilation, 66
vertical integration, 20
Vice President, 146, 151
victims, 48
Vietnam, v, vii, viii, 46, 131, 137
vision(s), 3, 10, 11, 15, 18, 22, 45, 55, 68, 80
vocabulary, 29
voicing, 139
volatile organic compounds, 61
voluntarism, 17
volunteers, 128
vulnerability, 145
vulnerable people, 137

W

wages, 139, 142, 147, 149, 150, 151, 152, 153, 154, 155, 156, 160
war, 45
warlords, 52
Washington, 150
waste, 1, 27, 61, 65, 66, 74, 100, 103
waste management, 1
waste treatment, 27
water, 1, 22, 23, 27, 53, 61, 65, 66, 80, 131, 139, 159, 160, 164
wealth, 1, 24, 32, 73, 75, 78, 137, 138
web, 28, 49
web service, 49
welfare, 52, 118, 149
wellbeing, 1, 18, 31, 45, 127, 132, 143, 145, 160
wellness, 165
Western Europe, 69
wildlife, 132
wind power, 66, 121
withdrawal, 21
wood, 66, 80
work ethic, 9
workers, 2, 6, 8, 11, 23, 56, 81, 96, 101, 121, 137-156, 159, 160, 162
workforce, 69, 74, 121, 128, 150, 151
working conditions, 6, 138, 140, 142, 151, 156
working hours, 139, 140, 143, 145, 147, 150, 153
workplace, 2, 141, 151, 162
World Bank, 25, 71
worldwide, 30, 31, 61, 68, 128, 131
worry, 143

Y

yield, 119, 137